Praise for Roberta Hill

"Time found its voice in the poetry of Roberta Hill. A powerful voice with the wings of Love and Death. A voice with the colors of ancient everyday landscapes and the colors of luminous dreams. *Cicadas: New & Selected Poems* by Roberta Hill is a must have, a must read and a must share with everyone."

—Moisés Villavicencio Barras, author of *Light of All Times*

"'I'm not first/ to go claim as kin/ the cicada.' In these poems spanning thirty years Roberta Hill chronicles the things that matter: family, the wisdom of animals, and the travails of 'this dancing earth.' In *Cicadas*, we watch the poet's journey from the landscapes of her youth to the hard-earned wisdom of the present. Ultimately Hill's poems are rife with the music that comes rising out of the soil. In short, *Cicadas* sings."

—Amy Quan Barry, author of *Water Puppets*

"With elegant rich imagery, these poems root deep in the memory of those who've gone before. Roberta Hill re-gifts us with the 'grace we lost' and reconnects us to our continuous presence on this continent, where we look out from the windows of these poems, in awe of the beauty unraveling before us."

—Sherwin Bitsui, author of *Flood Song*

T0151908

POETRY BOOKS BY ROBERTA HILL

Cicadas: New & Selected Poems (2013)

Philadelphia Flowers (1996)

Star Quilt (1984)

Cicadas

NEW & SELECTED
POEMS

Roberta Hill

HOLY COW! PRESS
DULUTH, MINNESOTA
2013

Book design by Anton Khodakovsky.

Printed and bound in the United States of America.

First printing, 2013

ISBN 978-0-9859818-0-8

10 9 8 7 6 5 4 3 2 1

This project is supported in part by grant awards from the Ben and Jeanne Overman Charitable Trust, the Elmer L. and Eleanor J. Andersen Foundation, the Cy and Paula DeCosse Fund of the Minneapolis Foundation, The Lenfestey Family Foundation, and by gifts from individual donors.

Holy Cow! Press books are distributed to the trade by Consortium Book Sales & Distribution, c/o Perseus Distribution, 210 American Drive, Jackson, TN 38301.

For inquiries, please write to:

Holy Cow! Press, Post Office Box 3170, Mount Royal Station, Duluth, MN 55803.

www.holycowpress.org

To the people, beings and places I love, named or unnamed,
met and imagined. May they continue to inspire
us to live and keep loving earth
and her beings
for all eternity.

Table of Contents

ACKNOWLEDGEMENTS

I wish to acknowledge and thank the editors of the following publications in which some of these poems first appeared:

From *Star Quilt*: *The American Poetry Review*; *First Skin Around Me: Contemporary American Tribal Poetry*; *The Nation*; *The North American Review*; *Poetry Northwest*; *The Southern Review*; *The Stream Invents a Smile*; *Voices of the Rainbow*; and *Where We Are: A Montana Poets Anthology*.

From *Philadelphia Flowers*: *Abraxis*; *Amicus Journal*; *An Ear to the Ground: An Anthology of Contemporary American Poetry*; *The Chariton Review*; *Common Ground: A Gathering of Poems on Rural Life*; *Early Ripening*; *Farm Women on the Prairie Frontier*; *Harper's Anthology of Twentieth-Century Native American Poetry*; *Kali-wesaks*; *North American Review*; *Tamaqua*; *Upriver Three*; *Wisconsin Academy Review*; *Wisconsin Dialogue*; and *Words in the Blood*.

From *Cicadas*: *The American Indian Culture and Research Journal*, for "Mother's Only Daughter," "At Lame Deer, Montana, "Cicada" and "Heat".

The Beloit Poetry Journal, for "Herbert Moon's Dilemma".

Cream City Review, for "Watching Folks Come Through," and "Before The Age of Reason".

Luna, for "Treatment," "Asking the Ocean God for Release at Myrtle Beach," and "The Whores of Telluride" .

Pemmican, for "In the Colonial Zone," "Conch," and "Cross-Section of Solitude".

Prairie Schooner, for "With Fog, Falling Earthward," and "Silences".

Re-inventing the Enemy's Language, edited by Joy Harjo and Gloria Bird (NY: W. W. Norton, 1997), for "To Rose," and "Waning August Moon".

Sister Nations, edited by Heid Erdrich and Laura Tohe, (St. Paul, MN: Minnesota Historical Society Press, 2002), for "Elegy for Bobby".

The Cold Mountain Review, for "Lights at Ray, Minnesota".

Valley Voices: A Literary Review, for "Getting Through".

Larry Alan Smith, conductor, Wintergreen Music Festival, for the musical performance of "Lane Tells Gladstone Belle His Story".

Star Quilt

1984

Star Quilt

These are notes to lightning in my bedroom.
A star forged from linen thread and patches.
Purple, yellow, red like diamond suckers, children

of the star gleam on sweaty nights. The quilt unfolds
against sheets, moving, warm clouds of Chinook.
It covers my cuts, my red birch clusters under pine.

Under it your mouth begins a legend,
and wide as the plain, I hope Wisconsin marshes
promise your caress. The candle locks

us in forest smells, your cheek tattered
by shadow. Sweetened by wings, my moth-like heart
flies nightly among geraniums.

We know of land that looks lonely,
but isn't, of beef with hides of velveteen,
of sorrow, an eddy in blood.

Star quilt, sewn from dawn light by fingers
of flint, take away those touches
meant for noisier skins,

anoint us with grass and twilight air,
so we may embrace, two bitter roots
pushing back into the dust.

Underground Water

"When spirit is heavy, it turns to water . . ."
—CARL JUNG

A child, awaking, takes the long way home.
Rain glistens on the window.
He hears voices abandoning weather. Narrow streams
trickle in the dark between streetlights
and a cloud folds down like a rag.
Down gutters, a dark field waits his escape.
There, birds flutter in the wet leaves
while clover blooms like the only stars.
A smell of mud skims through the room,
tired perfume on a blush of air.
A cat in heat asks its question
and tap water thumps its way alone.
As he walks by, the dresser creaks
and swirls of paint sigh like night blooming dahlias.

Cabbage moths dancing against his chin,
he pads to his parents' bed and crawls between them.
The sound of underground water rustles
like taffeta around their hips. It pulls him
toward the warmth of sea plums.
A birthmark of foam encircles his neck.
Listening in the quilted dark,
he slips away to another sun. From there,
he watches mother stare at a smoky bulb
in this last room. She'll never hear
the lilies rise, the weeds spin in the shallows
or water lap the half-awakened stones.
She hasn't words enough to lock his days.
They say goodbye on every heartbeat.

At every moment, dozens of water-birds
whir in flight, their quicksilver wings
confusing the leaves. Goodbye,
goodbye, the curtains breathe,
while memories, those stains on linen, remain
the last design. With bones of moonlight,
she skirts the water's edge. On her head,
a cap of fluttering voices. Cabbage moths,
her mad soul's journeymen, play in her hair.

Turning in her sleep, she feels again his breath
upon her cheek. Softer than the eye closing in death,
a curled leaf falls from his forehead
and is lost in the grass.

In the Longhouse, Oneida Museum

House of five fires, you never raised me.
Those nights when the throat of the furnace
wheezed and rattled its regular death,
I wanted your wide door,

your mottled air of bark and working sunlight,
wanted your smoke-hole with its stars,
and your roof curving its singing mouth above me.
Here are the tiers once filled with sleepers,

and their low laughter measured harmony or strife.
Here I could wake amazed at winter,
my breath in the draft a chain of violets.
The house where I lived as a child now seems

a shell of sobs. Each year I dream it sinister
and dig in my heels to keep out the intruder
banging at the back door. My eyes burn
from cat urine under the basement stairs

and the hall reveals a nameless hunger,
as if without a history, I should always walk
the cluttered streets of this hapless continent.
Thinking it best I be wanderer,

I rode whatever river, ignoring every zigzag,
every spin. I've been a fragment, less than my name,
shaking in a solitary landscape,
like the last burnt leaf on an oak.

What autumn wind told me you'd be waiting?
House of five fires, they take you for a tomb,
but I know better. When desolation comes,
I'll hide your ridgepole in my spine

and melt into crow call, reminding my children
that spiders near your door
joined all the reddening blades of grass
without oil, hasp or uranium.

Elegy for Jim White

You must have said *'yes'* this time,
yes to squeaks tucked in hotel rooms,
yes to rainwater trembling in the gutter,
yes to Aldebaran under clouds.

I thought I'd always find you here,
sitting at the breakfast table
while the notes of a distant dove
eased the shadow in your heart.

But when the poem rose from the page
and drifted toward eternity, you gazed
at your hand as it earned dexterity
from sunlight. You held the wings of dahlias.

All our imperfections remain.
They were your wealth. In your view,
the mold played equal to the night.
Once you said you were afraid

that dying meant no more birds,
no mud, no buses bouncing their patrons,
no sidewalks steaming in mid-July.
How right you were, my friend.

Although dying's never new,
your loss has worked a different world
where planets shape a sickle before dawn.
As Cassiopeia rocks to sleep, a husband

down the street drives home
in time to bleed. Underneath the sidewalk,
one fickle ant broods about last summer.
Since your death, the snow

carries more than she can name.
I wrap the wind inside my coat.
My blood blazes like a crystal.
May all these imperfections remain.

A Nation Wrapped in Stone

—for Susan Iron Shell

When night shadows slipped across the plain, I saw a man
beside his horse, sleeping where neither man nor horse
had been. I've prayed
to a star that lied. The spirits near the ceiling of your room,
did they leave on horseback, turning dew into threads
by moonlight?
In wild stretch of days, you didn't fear ashes or weeping.
We, left behind, can't warm sunlight.
Isaac, you left with the wind.

The chokecherry grows slower. I held your trembling wife,
and windows trembled in our north room. The creek gnaws
remaining snow. Our blood runs pale.
You taught us to be kind to one another. Now we wake, questioning
our dreams. Nighthawks in warm fog. A nation wrapped in stone.
What do nurses
know of hay, of scents that float broken between canyons,
of strength in a worn face? You wept love, not death.
Around your bed, owls stood.

The north wind hunts us with music, enough pain
to set fires in ancient hills. West winds growl
around Parmelee.

The tanned, uneven banks will hold more frost. Unlike dust,
we cannot die from tears. You've settled
on a quiet prairie. Shrouded eyes
in thickets give a reason to contain
this heavy rind. We are left with grief, sinking bone-ward,
and time to watch rain soak the trees.

Reaching Yellow River

"It isn't a game for girls,"
he said, grabbing a fifth
with his right hand,
the wind with his left.

"For six days
I raced Jack Daniels.
He cheated, told jokes.
Some weren't even funny.

That's how come he won.
It took a long time
to reach this Yellow River.
I'm not yet thirty,

or is it thirty-one?
Figured all my years
carried the same hard thaw.
Out here, houselights hid

deep inside the trees.
For awhile I believed this road
cut across to Spring Creek
and I was trucking home.

I could kid you now,
say I ran it clean,
gasping on one lung,
loaded by a knapsack

of distrust and hesitation.
I never got the tone
in all the talk of cure.
I sang Honor Songs, crawled

the railroad bridge to Canada.
Dizzy from the ties,
I hung between both worlds.
Clans of blackbirds circled

the nearby maple trees.
The dark heart of me said
no days more than these.
As sundown kindled the sumacs,

stunned by the river's smile,
I had no need for heat,
no need to feel ashamed.
Inside me then the sound

of burning leaves. Tell them
I tumbled through a gap on the horizon.
No, say I stumbled through a hummock
and fell in a pit of stars.

When rain weakened my stride,
I heard them singing
in a burl of white ash,
took a few more days to rave

at them in this wood.
Then their appaloosas nickered
in the dawn and they came
riding down a close ravine.

Though the bottle was empty,
I still hung on. Foxtails beat
the grimace from my brow
until I took off my pain

like a pair of old boots.
I became a hollow horn filled
with rain, reflecting everything.
The wind in my hand

burned cold as hoarfrost
when my grandfather nudged me
and called out
my Lakota name."

.   .   .

In memory of Mato Heholgeca's grandson

Overcast Dawn

This morning I feel dreams dying.
One trace is this feather
fallen from a gull,
with its broken shaft,
slight white down,
and long dark tip
that won't hold air.
How will you reach me
if all our dreams are dead?
Will I find myself
as empty as an image,
that death mask of a woman
reflected in car windows?
Help me, for every bird
remembers as it preens
the dream that lifted
it to flight.
Help me, for the sky
is close with feathers,
falling today
from sullen clouds.

Winter Burn

When birds break open the sky, a smell of snow
blossoms on the wind. You sleep, wrapped up
in blue dim light, like a distant leaf of sage.
I drink the shadow under your ear
and rise, clumsy, glazed with cold.
Sun, gleaming in frost, reach me.
Touch through the window this seed that longs
little by little to flare up orange and sing.
Branches turn to threads against the sun.
Help us to wake up, enormous space that makes
us waver, dark horizon that keeps us strong.

Your heart pours over this land, pours over memories
of wild plum groves,
laughter, a blur between leaves.
These fences hold back frost, let horses run.
Spirits hunt our human warmth
in these quiet rooms. Dogs follow us,
bark at the piercing air. I sort beans,
wish for something neither key nor hand can give.
I must watch you suffering the doubt and grace
of foxes. Let clear winter burn away my eyes.
Let this seed amaze the ground again.

Beside barrels, a mouse glares at me,
folding against the present like a draft against a flame.
Curious bitter eyes tick away
my years. Women have always heard this,
his rattle signaling a day brought wide
like slow ripples in a river.
Ask him why water drifts over moss.

Your hair grows fish-haunted. You are never warned.
Ask why those waving weeds steal what you become.
His answer, the slow tick of fire.
Near timber, axes sing inside the poles.

You chop wood and chop a buried city
from your bones. Far off, the clouds are floating into dusk.
We stack up logs traveling to the dry field
of our breath. Like ants, we pace the ground,
and let a strange heat shake our darkness,
an old web streams through the door.
Hushed steps follow you to valleys,
where, aching and ringing, you no longer want to look,
until, touching the sudden pulse of all we are,
you burn into the yellow grass of winter,
into one reed, trembling on the plain.

Midwinter Stars

The trees across the street have loved me
in your absence. The Pole star, caught by branches
of the front yard elm, blurs
when I look at it directly and passes
through midwinter slower than other stars.
Whenever you came by, the forest

filled with signs. A pocket in soft grass
meant resting deer. Hoofprints in the sand
lead through brush and fallen leaves
to even dimmer trails. I hated all my rooms.
The lonely light, absurd.
I warmed your shoulders one late November storm

and trees sang in minor chords.
Aware of dawn before it came, you woke,
smiled into clothes, juggled with coffee,
then drove away. I watched shadows turn
from indigo to grey.
Like other obsessions, this will change,

yet my arm was happy, numb
with all your weight. I learned the easy signs:
cloud cover, tracking snow.
I fell with every flake and wanted to drape
over trees, into city blocks, on those corners
where you bought beer, over cars and bridges

in that namesake of despair.
There are places I have never felt at ease,
where something taps against the glass,

the blackjack of a cop and bitter lives.
Who the hunter? Who the hunted? Who survives?
This cold circuit wobbles without rest.

I never could accept beginning or end.
You'll find on the other side of winter
crocus trembling in a bountiful dawn.
I plan to join the deer,
for in this dark, the trees bar my window
and not one shadow moves.

The Recognition

We learn too late the useless way light leaves
footprints of its own. We traveled miles to Kilgore
in the submarine closeness of a car. Sand hills
recalling the sea. A coyote slipped across the road
before we knew. Night, the first skin around him.
He was coming from the river
where laughter calls out fish. Quietly a heavy wind
breaks against cedar. He doubled back,
curious, to meet the humming moons we rode
in this gully, without grass or stars. Our footprints
were foreign to him. He understood the light
and paused before the right front wheel, a shadow
of the mineral earth, pine air in his fur.
Such dogs avoid our eyes, yet he recognized and held
my gaze. A being both so terrible and shy
it made my blood desperate
for the space he lived in:
broad water cutting terraced canyons,
and ice gleaming under hawthorn like a floor of scales.
Thick river, remember we were light thanking light,
slow music rising. Trees perhaps, or my own voice
out of tune. I danced a human claim for him
in this gully. No stars. He slipped
by us, old as breath, moving in the rushing dark
like moonlight through tamarack,
wave on wave of unknown country.
Crazed, I can't get close enough
to this tumble wild and tangled miracle.
Night is the first skin around me.

Blue Mountain

—for Richard Hugo

West of your door, Blue Mountain dreams of melting
to the sea. You wait a simple answer.
Tomorrow is a harvest.
I understand what roads you've climbed
in the tinted smoke of afternoon.
Crickets whir a rough sun into haze.
The thickly planted field invades your longing.

I left that mountain in easy goodbyes.
The moon flooding me home. The Garnet Range
like arms letting go moments
when too much talk grows fatal. Now
moss folds down in matted sleep. Watch
how wind burns lazily through maples.
I sweep and sweep these broken days to echoes.

More than land's between us. Wood smoke in the sun.
Timber shrinks below the bend.
Our walls stay thin. We trust them,
loving the light that bleeds around the shade.
Peepers show us why we live, astonished
at new frost. You taught me how to track
this ragged fire. Chickadees keep me going.

I've begged a place for you to come at last.
Clouds gather like mints. Warm, dancing like gnats
in sunshine, rain hugs your heavy arms. Your woman smiles.
The flint lake brightens. In the slow roll
of a wave, joy buries its weight deep
inside your lungs. One bird calls from a far-off pine.
You and Blue Mountain will reach the sea.

Seal at Stinson Beach

She asked brown eyes, "Burn me loose.
Unmask this loss of estuaries, lamp shells."
The lowland wheat dreams against moonlight
and empty houses creak their own tough joy.
On this wintry coast, remember how, in faint light,
Mother's eyes wore green, how
Eleanor sank. A trunk along flat pine.

Beyond breakers, a mute hunter floats, forgetful
of running sharks, sea moss. Teach me
your crisscross answer
to the cackling of gulls,
Closets can mend
sinister days, yet these losses hum
in the walls.

He swam a shadow, a blemish on the waves.
Is this the last year of tasting dust,
of violent wakings?
Blue sea-shot boils around my shoes. Breakers crash.
Hiss again. He leans, foreign as a star,
for places where the man-of-war
hangs its tendrils down.
In the drawing back, the breathing in, I find my bones.

Minor Invasions

It goes, yet isn't gone,
this dust invading my square of sun.
My mother saved her days until she died,
fighting these little boats
that break the monotony of sunlight.
She denied it fell from stars.
She called it dirt and did it in.
The highboy, always hungry for her touch,
swallowed with a blackness not of earth,
a necklace of feathers and cones,
a flower, love letter, favorite Easter egg.
All wasted things belonged in there.
Its dust was all mirage.

Dust knows the value of lost days,
days when do, do, do wrenches
from us too the screech of boxcars.
Memories work against us,
gathering that darkness inside the eye,
until winter roars its final white.
Now I let go, struggle with these moments
brought like waves, and feel them break
as soon as they are formed.
I let the long drawer of the past
swallow once again
the old photographs in whose relentless light
we both stood
without a speck of dust.

Dream of Rebirth

We stand on the edge of wounds, hugging canned meat,
waiting for owls to come grind
night-smell in our ears. Over fields,
darkness has been rumbling. Crows gather.
Our luxuries are hatred. Grief. Worn-out hands
carry the pale remains of forgotten murders.
If I could only lull or change this slow hunger,
this midnight swollen four hundred years.

Groping within us are cries yet unheard.
We are born with cobwebs in our mouths
bleeding with prophecies.
Yet within this interior, a spirit kindles
moonlight glittering deep into the sea.
These seeds take root in the hush
of dusk. Songs, a thin echo, heal the salted marsh,
and yield visions untrembling in our grip.

I dreamed an absolute silence birds had fled.
The sun, a meager hope, again was sacred.
We need to be purified by fury.
Once more eagles will restore our prayers.
We'll forget the strangeness of your pity.
Some will anoint the graves with pollen.
Some of us may wake unashamed.
Some will rise that clear morning like the swallows.

Patterns

If I could track you down to have you taste
the strawberry shaded by beggar's green,
the winter wheat, remote as sunlight
through low-moving clouds, we'd face
the squash blossom, fixed in its quiet temple,
and breathe in rhythm to our own beginnings.

Instead I step without your echo
over the cucumbers' tapestry of tendril
and wooly stem. The corn, my blind children,
mingle with wind and I walk naked
into their midst to let them brush my hips
with searching fingers, their cuffs alive with rain.

When I ask if they are happy,
a few by the fence whisper "Yes." It comes
through the rows, yes again
and again yes. My feet take root
in rings of corn light; the green earth
shouts more green against the weighted sky,

and under poppies of ash, patterns emerge:
lilacs collecting dark beneath the sheen of elms,
cedar buds tinting air with memories of frost,
a tanager's cry deep inside the wind break,
my life's moiré of years. When my jailors,
these brief words, fumble with their bony keys,

I listen to the arguments of flies, to the long
drawn-out call of doves, for lessons in endurance.
Moths, twilight in their wings,

dance above the oat leaves,
and I know you stand above the same muted sea,
brooding over smoke that breaks
around hollyhock's uneven pinnacles.

For a moment, we are together,
where salt-stunted trees glory in the sun, where verbena
and jasmine light the wind with clean tomorrows.
I felt us there, felt myself and not-myself there.
We lived those promises ridiculed in solemn days.
We lived with a hunger only solitude can afford.

Climbing Gannett

While you clambered up ahead,
jabbing a staff into chunks of snow,
I rested on a rock shelf, wedded
to my breath, to ridges and plateaus,
careening blue and bluer,
to aspens below, flickering
in a downhill draft.

Lengthening its hollows,
the teal blue peak above us
made you laugh. Never did you feel
as close as then,
straddling the distant slope,
balancing in cold wind.
As you climbed beyond my help,

a rim of the crevasse broke to foam.
I heard your wild echo.
"It's no storm." When the mountain
hurled boulders across the sky,
your face blazed in the close grey air,
then the slide pulled you
with a roar, whirring loud

and long, like the wing beats
of a hundred hawks. Although I held on,
my life leapt at your glance.
I held on for weeks, for weeks I walked
the crumbling fields. In the homeland
of ravens, I stroked the shadow
of each gangling pine, and measured

the distance to your grave.
Across the vista, other peaks darkened.
You were swept away so suddenly.
Surely you'll tap,
perhaps below that copper ridge,
or in that far ravine,
I dream on the icy plain.

Nameless and alone, I sang
in the yellow light of a lily,
and woke to welcome you,
bound by a miniature range.
Outside our window, a warbler claims
another dawn. Do you think
the light drove away that colder wind?

Made of Mist

I stumbled on each step as I went down
to hear the water, rumbling on my left,
to see the rocks, creating a shelf
with bright colors streaked in red and brown.

Isolated in a big, black rubber coat,
I heard the wind, but could
the wind hear me, sitting aft
and singing as the boat

dropped from dock and churned on churning waves?
Warm sun and mist rolled over every face.
Lovers locked their elbows and changed place.
I walked along the rail. The engine slaved

along the falls, ferns hiding a lair
where a snake lay twisted into stone.
Tomorrow, even this, a darkened wound.
A thousand gulls charmed that frantic air

and I have never felt that kind of love.
Lost in wing beat,
in heavy spray, wanting to meet
their frail lament, I moved

to the front where motion bound with praise
was the whole world,
and I have yet to stop being swirled
through the dark and light of coming days.

Mother

Once I tried to build you out of boxes,
but none had the proper warmth
and I can't remember how you lugged
laundry to the line or tied your apron.
I was the one who watched you sob
in rhythm with the treadle,
the needle traveling over the tweed
for my new coat.

You drugged me so I'd sleep all night,
but still I wandered down
that deep blue sleeve to your room,
crawled between you and Dad
where a garden grew under moth-soft blankets.
Chinaberry trees bathed me in green
while phlox and windflower
leaned into my life. There,
too, the guinea hens of your stories
hunkered in the dirt.

Tucking mothballs in the blankets
one morning, you found silence heaped
behind winter coats in the closet.
Quivering, you kept this to yourself,
but grew more optimistic as you died,
planning rides in the park,
the next picnic, and frequently telling us
we'd like the way
Spanish moss trembles in acacia trees
when we travel south.

Tiptoeing down the hall, we found
a translucent shell curled
in your sheets. Attendants took you
to a cleaner room, rendered your shape
a channel for sunlight. Mother,
your mouth was always pursed
slightly open as you slept.
Between drunken ghosts,
I've listened to that bell for years.

Tempered by your trembling chin,
your hot last kiss,
I knew at nine
that love and death were equal
and that no one was left
to whip such notions
from my unforgiving hide.

Woman Seed Player

—for Oscar Howe

You balanced her within a cyclone
and I believe the young wind
that frequents the graveyard
tugs her sleeve. Her hand never wavers,
though the stakes are always high.

When running shadow turns rattler,
her concern is how the mountain rises
beyond its line of sorrow. Then,
shooting her seeds, she bids
the swallow fly over rolling hills.

I have been obsessed with permanence.
Struggling in that space under every word,
I've heard exuberant waves drift
denying limitations. Last April
when we trudged upstairs

to where we found you sketching,
you said no one has ever gone full circle,
from passion through pattern and back again
toward pebbles moist with moonlight.
How easily the rain cross-stitches

a flower on the screen, quickly
pulls the threads, varying the line.
Many times this year, I've watched that player
play. She doesn't force the day
to fit her expectations.

Now she pulls me through.
The leaf light dust and her stable hand
allow my will its corner of quiet.
Watch dust embracing the nervous wheat;
every throw's a different combination.

Dust whirs brighter in the door jam,
one last uproar before the rain.
Her bundle contains and yet forgoes
the dark dust already fallen for tomorrow
from long-since gentle stars.

Inspired by "Woman Seed Player," a painting by Oscar Howe

Lynn Point Trail

That rare day we played for real
and left traces of our walking sticks
in last year's leaves. Lynn Point Trail
hid us in rushing green, in the quick
dark of Douglas fir where death conceals
itself in blazing moss.

Leading us in the journey,
our children stomp-danced until the ferns
bristled with the authority
of hooded cobras. When they turned
to us for answers, we began to see
fronds tremble with a delicate weight,

as if infinity had stirred the stem.
The scattered light peopled each ravine.
We longed for woods this deep, for this glen
where you knelt to photograph a gleam
inside a bridge of stone. Was it then
Missy wouldn't go on?

Our youngest girl wanted to believe
home could be this emerald grotto.
Nearby, we heard the breaking sigh of waves,
while, bickering in a bird's staccato,
she kept her gesture firm, though naïve:
Here we belonged.

A cuckoo's call echoed in the sun.
I, too, wish we could have lived
near the tilted horizon,
close to the fluttering mat that weaves
dun fly and dune into one.

With songs for granite and bluer skies,
our children gathered rain-eroded shells.
Let these rocks be eggs until the tides
scorch them, or until the heart reveals
at last the grace we lost.

Philadelphia Flowers

1996

Dreaming in Broad Daylight

Rising in the quiet dark, the morning star takes
the torturous errors of this haunted world
and changes them to wings. My adolescence clings

like a burr against my heart. In this life,
we walk a spiral way and must return
to that ecstasy burning in our youth.

Sometimes when you stand in the corridor
of my dreams, your black eyes awaken
forgotten rhythms in my blood.

I long to escape to the sea, for only
the hiss, the crash of the surf can stop my dreaming
in broad daylight. I see the roof collapse.

The wind breaks through the rafters,
but you, steady as a boulder in the ruins,
continue to make me bloom amid destruction.

You are a gargoyle, a guardian from far south,
who keeps me from despair in this year
when we rekindle the fire of compassion.

We live on separate levels and never touch,
yet I must suffer the lightning you bring
when you point to a gap in the roof

from which we watch the precession of stars.
In a time before time took you, I felt
your leaving. Not in your gait, nor those black eyes,

but in your smile and ready laugh, death relayed
an ancient message. Was your loneliness the length
of mountain road where they beat you to a grave?

Now when I wake, though I never wake completely,
some of that same grace drives me toward compassion.
I see it in the trees, glistening deep green in half-dark.

Our lives linger on the outer edge of night
from where such knowledge comes. Birds flutter and sing,
as the morning star spills wind across our world.

Where I Come From

Even native peoples who have been here 25,000 years
were probably immigrants from Asia.
—LUCY R. LIPPARD

Intricate energies of our roots on Turtle Island
have supported us. It's difficult to accept
how long we've been here. In the pulse
of my daily life, ancient spirits send

sunlight winking through leaves.
With horns of wisdom and feathered arms,
they travel swiftly, dazzle me and lift
my sorrow. Intimate with this earth,

we pay attention. In wind blasting treetops
before the first summer rain, in the night sky
wide with stars and from those images ancestors
pecked into cliffs and onto stones,

these spirits come to quicken us with a presence
as unsettling as mountain shadows.
I come from the red earth of Turtle Island.
This earth has always been our home.

My ancestors were not immigrants from Asia.
Twenty-five thousand years ago, they
didn't trudge over the MacKensie Corridor
in search of more wooly mammoths.

The one who gives us life, mind, and blood
has enclosed his vision and breath in our bodies,
so we might add to this beauty.
We were not created to atone

for some long ago mistake.
We were not made to beg from another's bowl,
or to control the ancient energies of earth.
The one whose beauty drifts in clouds,

whose voice rises from the thrush
in its tangle of brambles,
whose power attracts us to the sigh
and surge of the sea, asked that we

add to this beauty and be grateful for each day.
We are glad we still remember
how to make with our hands, our eyes, our voices,
these forms, these visions, these songs.

Waterfall at Como Park

She's always walking off the edge,
allowing the wellspring of herself
to fall away without worry.

Even in a furious wind, she's out there,
shaking her glinting spray across the sandstone.
Through thick August afternoons,

she gazes at the sky and stays
poised enough to welcome sparrows.
Both structure and flux, she trembles

as she collects pebbles and leaves, while
her basin grows deeper, more substantial.
Those days when love is distant,

I return to her and learn how she sinks,
climbs and leaps into abundant moments
where she gives without purpose

or boundary. She teaches me to believe
in this—it's best we're blind
to that which moving, moves us.

In her great-hearted leaps, she's my anchor,
gathering shadow and sun
without once stopping her song.

Acknowledgement

*"I fight so they will recognize me and
treat me like a human being."*
—RIGOBERTA MENCHU

Listen, for the Lord
of the Near and Close comes
to make you see
in steam rising from coffee,
smoke from bodies burning in Panzos.
Sometime he'll have you taste
in your chocolate bars
that bitterness children carry
when they dare not bury
their bludgeoned mothers.

On the backs of owls,
Izquic, Woman's Blood, flew
out of smoldering hells,
carrying within her twins
who restored freedom
to those sunlit mountains.
Sometime she'll have you smell
in the red and fragrant flowers
hearts of boy soldiers,
hanging in trees.

Where is the Mirror
That Makes all Things Shine?
The night wind's my Lord.
He cleans the bodies flung in ravines,
and comforts aching women,

standing before their fragile fires.
His breath's a spiral
wide as this galaxy
where nothing is obscured.

Obsidian Butterfly will force you to see
how children sleep in a cardboard box
year after tremulous year. In the span
of their hands, onions, gruel, and
a dangerous abyss
for the people of this sun.
In clouds and mist, their suffering moves.

Something comes to wake you.
Something comes without faltering
Can you feel it in the twilight?
In your fruits and in your cheeses,
in your signatures?
The gods and goddesses are talking together,
scanning dumpsters and smog,
nuclear playgrounds. They soothe
cholera-stricken geese and the broken
feet of coyotes.

In their diminishing forests
they meet, counting the heartbeats
it will take to make
each face sublime.
Will you acknowledge the love
and faith of our restless earth,
or will you claim the suffering's
too far south while your mouth
samples and measures, calls everything
tangible?

Through darkness, through night
our suffering moves,
a slow quake in the chest, a sigh.
No food and the body will eat itself.
Some of you bluster and do not believe
we have cut the heart of the sky.
You give gasoline to the lords
of your death,
spoon out the sugar,
ignoring its tears.

One More Sign

—in memory of Norbert Seabrook Hill

Last night I dreamed you drank coffee
in my kitchen. After telling me of Teapot Dome,
how you roamed by boxcar
through the thirties, you blew four times
in your left fist, nodding at the hiss
of snow outside the screen. One more sign
an island will rise in the Caribbean.

Peering through our earthly dark, you laugh
when I say we won't find you again.
When I explain you cannot be here,
you hitch your belt in back, balancing
that rubber ball above a wound from World War II.
You grip the cup as you once did a drill,
then rise and quickly drink it down.

My uncle, I reach for an embrace,
but brimming through that space, cedar smoke
and the language of rain, lost in its
soliloquy. We didn't listen closely enough
to those rim world people singing in the pines.
We didn't thrill at the wind,
racing through a rhombus of stars.

You knew how secret influences—
leaf, stone, web—converge upon a life
and keep it fed with wonder.
Let others suspect you of false dreams,
an old man speaking to the cosmos
with a pendulum of keys. We whirled
unaware you were the balance wheel.

A week before you left, I thought
you the man crossing Barstow.
On the other side of the street, he
became a stranger, digging in his pocket
for change to buy a paper. Then I feared
your spirit traveled while you catnapped
in a room. Television glow. Closer zoom.

That day you danced away
air around Oneida held such moxie
it lingers on the ridges yet,
incandescent blue. The beating drum.
The beating heart. The galaxy's great arm
sparkled closer with each step
until the heart you often hit
to start again refused. I wait for you
to visit me in dreams. Some moments,
it seems I only need to call
to ask how ball players will arrive
from their court beneath the waves.
Even now, I listen in the dawn
to voices, calm, subterranean.

From The Sun Itself

While something hummed along the river,
I sat on a wooded hill in Spring,
playing my flute to fluttering green.
At my feet, a bellwort and a fern.

A white pine churned above me.
From the sun itself, the bellwort's flame.
An oak branch snapped, then crashed behind me,
as he came through the canopy.

A huge hawk folded, fell, then opening
his mantle, swooped under oaks with no qualm.
With the mastery of ashes, he twisted, lifted
and turned, breezing easily on broad wings.

I clung to a high note, more for my health
than his. No stranger to the scheming wind,
he hit the rim of the hill, flicked
his red tail and broke into blue.

The mottled light underneath his wings
scattered into beeches below.
Heady with flight, I stood silent, for
he knew what the human heart renounces.

He circled east and flew to the sun itself.
So drawn to him by my longing,
I didn't hear the deepening drone.
As bellwort, fern and pine bough grew greener,

the chopper's keen blade lagged for a moment,
after a dawn raid on the gypsy moths.
The pilot may never know he was swinging
the fierce edge of our twilight.

Against Annihilation

— for Jacob A. Hill

When I found eraser dust
from "You must do your math"
left on my desk this morning, I thought of how
I love to see your face,
at once so familiar, so foreign.
Soon, you will be a man
in a country born from war,
in a country that renews its pride
by making cluster-bombs. But this morning
we are safe on our street and I can watch
your spirit shimmer around you
when you laugh.

At this moment, the joy of antelope twins
who bounded before you on the day
of your birth overtakes you.
You grow bold, curious
to the point of danger,
tramping through jack pines,
setting up camps. Your nomadic soul
follows the wind's way—
whatever arrives, arrives.
Yet you never stay out too long

before the coolness of the turtle clan
glides over your shoulders.
Then your turtle heart hedges
and you hoard string,
bits of tin, railroad ties,
like gatherers who abided
under ancient maples.

You grow so hard on yourself, hibernating,
building robots in your room,
your blood blooming under dreaming seas,
inaccessible to me,
though at times like these
you stand before an open window
like my father.

At such moments, do you ponder
just what phenolphthalein means?
This poem asks the earth
to offer you her care,
to remind you that your grandfathers
lived here for five hundred thousand years.
They followed The Loon,
so it may also guide
your running through the humming night.

At distances greater than your twelve years,
through the silhouettes
of starker fears, may these blessings
find you still
wonderously alive
in this world that prizes
annihilation.

Philadelphia Flowers

I

In the cubbyhole entrance to Cornell and Son,
a woman in a turquoise sweater
curls up to sleep. Her right arm seeks
a cold spot in the stone to release its worry
and her legs stretch
against the middle hinge.

I want to ask her in for coffee,
to tell her to go sleep in the extra bed upstairs,
but I'm a guest,
unaccustomed to this place
where homeless people drift along the square
bordering Benjamin Franklin Parkway.

From her portrait on the mantel,
Lucretia Mott asks when
will Americans see
how all forms of oppression blight
the possibilities of a people.
The passion for preserving Independence Square

should reach this nameless woman, settling
in the heavy heat of August,
exposed to the glare of every passerby.
What makes property so private? A fence?
No trespassing signs? Militia ready to die for it
and taxes? Light in the middle stories

of office buildings blaze all night above me.
Newspapers don't explain how wealth

is bound to these broken people.
North of here, things get really rough.
Longshoremen out of work bet on eddies
in the Schuylkill River.

Factories collapse to weed
and ruptured dream. Years ago, Longhouse sachems
rode canoes to Philadelphia,
entering these red brick halls.
They explained how
the law that kept them unified

required a way to share the wealth.
Inside the hearths of these same halls,
such knowledge was obscured,
and plans were laid to push all Indians
west. This city born of brotherly love
still turns around this conflict.

Deeper in the dusk,
William Penn must weep
from his perch on top of City Hall.
Our leaders left this woman in the lurch.
How can there be democracy
without the means to live?

II
Every fifteen minutes
a patrol car cruises by. I jolt awake
at four a.m. to sirens screeching
and choppers lugging to the hospital heliport
someone who wants to breathe.

The sultry heat leads me
to the window. What matters? This small
square of night sky and two trees
bound by a wide brick wall.
All around, skyscrapers

are telling their stories
under dwindling stars. The girders
remember where Mohawk iron workers stayed
that day they sat after work
on a balcony, drinking beer.

Below them, a film crew caught
some commercials. In another room above
a mattress caught fire and someone flung it
down into the frame. A woman in blue
sashayed up the street

while a flaming mattress,
falling at the same speed as a flower,
bloomed over her left shoulder.
Every fifteen minutes
a patrol car cruises by. The men inside

mean business. They understood the scene.
A mattress burning in the street
and business deadlocked. Mohawks
drinking beer above it all.
They radioed insurrection,

drew their guns, then three-stepped
up the stairs. Film crews caught the scene,
but it never played. The Mohawks

didn't guess a swat team had moved in.
When policemen blasted off their door,

the terrified men shoved a table
against the splintered frame.
They fought it out.
One whose name meant Deer got shot
again and again. They let him lie

before they dragged him by his heels
down four flights of stairs. At every step,
he hurdled above his pain
until one final leap
gained him the stars.

The news reported one cop broke his leg.
The film's been banished to a vault. There are
no plaques. But girders whisper at night
in Philadelphia. They know the boarding house,
but will not say. They know as well what lasts
and what falls down.

III

Passing Doric colonnades of banks
and walls of dark glass,
passing press-the-button-visitors-please
Liberty Townhouses, I turned
up Broad Street near the Hershey Hotel
and headed toward the doorman
outside the Bellevue. Palms and chandeliers inside.
A woman in mauve silk and pearls stepped into the street.
I was tracking my Mohawk grandmother
through time. She left a trace

of her belief somewhere near Locust and Thirteenth.
I didn't see you, tall, dark, intense,

with three bouquets of flowers in your hand.
On Walnut and Broad, between the Union League
and the Indian Campsite, you stopped me,
shoving flowers toward my arm.

"At least, I'm not begging," you cried.
The desperation in your voice
spiraled through my feet while I fumbled the few bucks
you asked for. I wanted those flowers—

iris, ageratum, goldenrod and lilies—
because in desperation
you thought of beauty. I recognized
the truth and human love you acted on,

your despair echoing my own.
Forgive me. I should have bought more
of those Philadelphia flowers, passed hand
to hand so quickly, I was stunned a block away.

You had to keep your pride, as I have done,
selling these bouquets of poems
to anyone who'll take them. After our exchange,
grandmother's tracks grew clearer.

I returned for days, but you were never there.
If you see her — small, dark, intense,
with a bun of black hair and the gaze of an orphan,
leave a petal in my path.
Then I'll know I can go on.

IV

Some days you get angry enough
to question. There's a plan out east
with a multitude of charts and diagrams.

They planned to take the timber, the good soil.
Even now, they demolish mountains.
Next they'll want the water and the air.

I tell you they're planning to leave our reservations
bare of life. They plan to dump their toxic
wastes on our grandchildren. No one wants to say

how hard they've worked a hundred years.
What of you, learning how this continent's
getting angry? Do you consider what's in store for you?

Letting Go

Under Blue Dome
where mountain spirits wander,
he curls in a green bedroll,
listening, listening
thirteen years old.

When the tent flap flutters,
he remembers T. J. stuffing gorp
into his backpack,
the grizzly snorting all night
through their camp in Sequoia,
until the dawn ranger reported:
Bear disturbance. No one injured.

In a wind-swollen flash
of sparks and ash, I hope he hears
a mountain spirit dancing nearby,
her stony breath pressing him
as much as the womanly night.

I had to let him go,
my gangly eagle child, struggling
to ride currents of life's uplifting wind,
yet then, as now and always,
when pines mimic ocean swells,
I want his radiant childhood
to carry him back to me,
like phosphorus returning
to a warm southern sea.

Even though
night's rapture grows between us,
each time he telephones,
distant as my own myth of mountains,
I listen for
the shift in tone
that tells me he's encountered
his true mother.

At daybreak
her iridescent song
drifts from a canyon
hidden in our dreams,
and we seem to rise from our own power,
so skilled is her vision.

I had to let him go
encounter his true father
in rings of evenstar shine and boulders.
Perched on a limb
of a salt-rimmed tree,
watching the heavy sea brighten
as twilight grows,
I hope he'll learn manhood needs
both action and repose.

How I long to save him
from the miseries of war.
Enough have died so far
in this quest for empire.

His true parents strengthen
his willingness to love,

his high-strung mirth
in the boardwalk's glare,
his dragging T. J.
from the undertow.

Cicadas flutter their flimsy
but persistent wings, until the buzzsaw
of their passion stings the July heat.

As storm clouds rise
and rain pommels oaks,
I notice in a lightning flash
the road's grown thin.
Suffering this sea change,
I peek again from the kitchen window.
Every light is on,
every curtain, open.

Van Gogh in the Olive Grove

"We do not know what will happen to us tomorrow,
but whatever it may be, think of me, think of me."
—Vincent Van Gogh

You walked into the olive grove
outside St. Remy
and knew you lied about everything
but this—only someone brave
could stand among these trees
that know how deep the wounds we give
ourselves. Once again the sun
struck root into your bones.
Once again you felt flung against this earth
and reeling still.

Reeling from an illness that overtook
your will, you drew a cipher in the shadow
and listened to the ancient conversation
of olive leaves and wind.
Is that why you painted them
bunched around themselves,
nodding like normal men
around a dining table?

Each one who walks alone
feels the same trick of sunlight.
In that suspended moment before dark,
shadows winnow amethyst wings
through the burnished grasses.

Did you sense a spark, a warning
from within, before you cracked apart
like glass flung in a furnace? On your sleeve,
a cicada clings, brown ship of earth
against the sunlight's sting.

You grieved for the decline and decadence
of things. "Adieu!" the great sun cries,
stroking your stubbled face,
changing hue each degree it fell.
Energies in your arm exalted that whirlpool,
broke through certain barriers, gaits and walls
to graft an apparition to our world.

I found the hidden path you painted in the grove.
Mountains waver on the rim like a mirage.
Sometimes in the woods, the sun grabs hold
of me. Then I hear light sizzling in the leaves
and feel ciphers wedged inside each stone.

Then every bit of dirt or stem glistens
as I do inside the sun. When this feeling comes,
I think of you in the olive grove,
taking in the wealth of those few trees,
the mountain farther than anyone believes.
I've lied about everything, but this.

Empress Hsaio-Jui
Speaks Her Mind

These last ten years
I didn't see our love dance in candlelight.
All this time we've been walking
down the dark halls
toward our tomb. Every gesture
born of love lights ten thousand candles.
In that light, Wanli,
Emperor of the Middle Kingdom,
the keystone of the arch
is poised above your head.

When you glanced at me
that moment, I found more riches
than the Phoenix cap of woven gold
or the jade cup whose handles
claw my heart.
First Empress Hsaio-Ching married your jade
and marble and I, the minor wife,
a green sea-mist hovering in your hazel eyes.
When no one else walks near,
you take my hand and lead me
underground. Sometimes we crawl
along the passages of this tomb, burdened
by afterimages of artisans dying
where they dreamed your greater glory.

Drunk inside silk curtains,
you trace our childhoods
with your finger on my belly.

Could you deny the cosmos
which declared you emperor at ten
and me your concubine?
In our next lives, let's be wrens
chirping in the cedars near this tomb,
flitting over the raked sand
in light like that under our lagoon.
Two wrens flying from Tiger
to Dragon Mountain.
Common spring birds
only a foreigner would notice.

No, you say. Impossible.
For childhood's lightest step
and greatest dread accompanies
each gesture even after we are dead
and these mahogany coffins hold us.
You saw dragons soaring
above the blue roof tiles of your temple
last month when you offered the first grain.
You're certain that great wheel of stars
above anticipates your claim
to create this beauty
at the cost of thirty thousand lives.

Wanli, you win
for you are emperor. Besides, you make me
delight in the glow
of a thousand times ten thousand
flames calmly consuming the wick
of our lives. You also want the two of us
to fly. A dragon and two phoenixes
whirl toward the summer sun,

while courtesans left below
smell the perfume we leave, rising.
Lights left from our love
will tremble in the draft.

Which of our longings
will the great wheel grant us?
Wanli, you laugh
tempting my elbow
with your yellow sleeve
again.

Storm Warning

On torrid summer nights,
when weathermen warn of whirlwinds,
of severe storms,
newly born, southwest of your streetlight,
welcome the rain and dance. Run out
in the cold spray, open your arms
so rain will run over your palms,

into your armpits. Welcome the rain
and dance. Leap over lawns
in your pajamas, lean into crescendos
of wind, eyelids fluttering,
hair unraveling with every lunge.
Let neighbors cower in the southwest corner,
pondering their insurance.

Your assurance rides with rain,
so stomp through puddles, spin in rhythm
with thunders. Lightning will loosen
that hard ache in your shoulders, the grasses
growing spongy under your feet, your spry step
veering over the vestibules
of earthworms.

Welcome the rain and dance. Feel summer
surge through your thighs as thunder booms
with longing for his full length of sky.
If wind wants your house,
let him have it. Look up as you whirl
through the storm. Feel these warm blessings
falling straight down.

Preguntas

—for Professor Hernan Vidal

In the classroom at Folwell Hall
while the afternoon sun warmed
the oak panels around us,
you said, "Your bones contain your people's history."
I had to write it down.
In my home state,
in Medford, Wisconsin, there is a bounty
for brown women like me.

The sign at the local pizzeria
announces "The First Annual Indian Shoot."
I felt the bones in my fingers
and I scruffed them across the sign.
"It is not the first," the right fingerbones sang.
"It has never been annual," the left ones added.

To some in this classroom, I may look
like a deer
or a quail preening in the back corner of the room
against the wall and window.
I warble in the air of the classroom,
Ok, Ok, I'll be that bird,
la guarda barranca who lives in these ravines
on the underside of American history.

From these thickets,
in the shadow of his years,
my father sits at our table
near the window telling stories.

The west wind knew how to listen
and sometimes sends his voice back to me
whenever my blood falters.

I welcomed his singing
in the dark, his sobbing
in the dark, paralyzed at times
in his struggle against the daily snare
of being declared worthless.

Because of him, I know
my flesh is corn come from earth.
Because of him, I know
my body is a hologram
of all that is and ever was.
What fear drives them?
What makes them want to annihilate
these memories in our bones and blood?

Bones breaking silence, speak.
Words finding wings, fly.
Wings bringing clouds, whirl.
Clouds bearing rain, fall
on those fields that uphold justice.

You taught me to consider the greater scene
where the process plays into deaths
we can't deny. They want hurt and rage
to cement our bones, so we can't dance by them.
They want us drunk and armed
whenever we ride across northern Wisconsin.
They'll call us terrorists and savages,
call newsmen to see

our hides tacked to garage doors
because we question the word "civilized"
openly against this treeless horizon,
because we declare ourselves
original human beings.

Sometimes across your face
floats a cloud of loneliness and loss,
of solidarity with those who suffer.
You draw schema on the blackboard
to reveal the wheel of fragments
in which we live. Although you clearly
show us contradictions like gears,
grinding every one of us into sand,
the schema have not taught me as much
as the sundown cloud across your face
when you speak of justice.

You have helped me understand
their fear of the dark
is not my identity.
Their Indian Shoot doesn't create
more wiggle room for a few more fish.
It's not about fish, but fake blue lakes.
Not about trees, but copper.

Sometimes the wind brings to my window
my father's voice with the voices of others.
Akwesasne, Tlaltelolco, Lac du Flambeau,
El Salvador. Because of you, I trust
bones breaking silence will speak,
words finding wings will fly,
wings bringing clouds will whirl,

and whirling clouds,
filled with oblique rain,
will fall on those fields
that answer these questions
of justice.

The Earth and I are One

I

Out of the layers of stars,
one star whose fragrance fills the wind
    comes dancing.
Out of the layers of air,
the sun, our brother, flies.
We are wrapped in his wings.
His golden glances hurls us spiraling
through space
    through time
        through dark.

In dawn light we walk gratefully
    in a living world.
The living wind breathes us,
moves in and out,
    spins in and out, up and
through spaces in the blue,
spaces where the fading stars twinkle back.

Shadows lengthen and grow bold.
The day unwinds his hair
and sets out on the open road.
Each day, a new vision,
    clouds and ravines,
        blue wind and buds.

II

Now grasses, blue, green,
jolt us with their reach,
pushing through the leaf mold
    to tremble with the urgent energy
        of their soft
            bristling songs.

These grasses beguile the geese
    northward, northward.
Now let us rest in their long touch,
let their delight shimmer over us,
until we too unfurl ourselves
    through this living world.

Under a blaze of maples,
under birches shaking their catlins,
under white pine's massive buoyancy,
over strawberries ripening,
over these hills echoing
    with buds and gusts of rain,
let us walk gratefully in this living
    world again.

Morning Talk

—for Melissa L. Whiteman

"Hi, guy," said I to a robin
perched on a pole in the middle
of the garden. Pink and yellow
firecracker zinnias, rough green
leaves of broccoli,
and deep red tomatoes on dying stems
frame his still presence.

"I've heard you're not
THE REAL ROBIN. Bird watchers have
agreed," I said. "THE REAL ROBIN
lives in England. They claim
you are misnamed and that we ought
to call you 'a red-breasted thrush'
because you are
indigenous."

He fluffed up. "Am I not
Jis ko ko?" he cried, "that persistent
warrior who carries warmth
northward every spring?"
He seemed so young, his red belly
a bit light and his wings, still
faded brown. He watched me
untangling the hose to water squash.

"Look who's talking!" he chirruped.
"Your people didn't come
from Europe or even India.

The turtles say you're a relative
to red clay on this great island."

Drops of crystal water
sparkled on the squash.

"Indigenous!" he teased
as he flew by.

A Presence That Found Me Again, Again

Wild plum red as ever
along the river this summer I fade
from my thirties
Roaring across the flats ten years ago
I caught you glowing
In spite of my spume of road dust
watching me
little sun setting in violet leaves
bell ringing in the sea-green dusk
to one moving without moorings
to one singing as she sank
into dark piny canyons

Wild plum ripe as ever
along the river even then
you invited faith in feeling
offered me a time when the sky gleamed
blue as my first mother's milk
buoyed me over swamp and coulee
like notes of a long lost melody
When I gleaned grief
you, another reaper, shook your red
skirt in leafy shadows

Wild plum red as ever
hanging on the warm edge of summer wind
the road mica bright
doors of sunlit haze
corn stubble

a gold procession against the shore
like long mornings before grief

I couldn't find my crossing
oaks trembled in their turning
smitten by that second most beautiful being
we call death
I couldn't find half my life
until you held me
a tremulous ripple left

in your branches

and wind just awakening
for his rounds

No Longer

I no longer fear the firestorm despair.
Green earth has coaxed my soul
over a blue bridge of forget-me-nots,
into her hollow of oak leaves, lilies.
Now each creek I cross balances
dark and day as birds gave no thought
to each wing's weight, but fly, singing.

I no longer expect the firestorm despair
to sear the ground I grow on.
Horns of sumac have broken my blindness.
Thunder's taste glitters on my lips.
The moon urges my blood root's burgeoning.
Her fierce song cools this light I feed on.
Together we travel this river of fervid stars.

Wherever in Winter

Wherever in winter you go, child,
I hope our prayers flutter behind you in the wind.
The moon's waxing toward a quarter with Venus
shining to its east. Together
they'll travel this January night, crossing each other
at the horizon in a cold moment before dawn.
By that time, you may be crossing for home.

I've asked each tree,
each tower of steel and glass,
each shrub along the alleys if they've seen you passing by.
Without a word, you disappeared
quickly into these quaking cities.
I wake at four a.m., feeling wind blowing
in every room. No one on earth has yet
helped me understand
this bare sadness rushing through dark halls.
Did my father feel this same anxiety,
staring at the blue of his bedroom
on those nights when the smell
of mud and rain filled me with an energy
I never could deny?

I tell myself stories about the prodigal,
the youthful immortals of Asia,
the restless coyote sniffing a pile of snow and shit.
Tomorrow you'll look
from a window where people rush to work,
and perhaps in that moment find the red road
and a friend.

Someone will surely say that is
her child, I recognize the face, and when they ask,
you'll call. I keep faith that wherever you are,
spirits of this earth and sky keep you aware
of how we are related to everything here.

Speaking With Mother

—for Rebecca Belmour

In combers breaking on the shore,
she leaves a line of foam with parting waves.
She's always answered me when I have asked,
although her answers never stay.
She loves a crowded place
and many views. At any water's edge,
I find her scribbling whispers.
"Every action that you take," she says,
"makes a whirlpool. Each blow
and each caress begins a pattern
I expand inside your cells.
Even in your gossamer souls,
you spin my rhythms."

In mountains, her voice sweeps
through every tree. On their bark,
her messages remain,
patterns not copying themselves
exactly. She enjoys transforming
root, worm and human bone. Mother, some
have hurt you with their greed,
with poisons they must make
for yellow ingots. "The greatest arrogance,"
she laughs, "begins when they ignore
what their feelings indicate.
So, I send a rain of rotting fish
or shake my plates to make the girders pop."

Some autumn evening, let's curl up
to watch her change
the hues in moonlit clouds.
Though breath and blood and bone keep
dialogues, oppression
has kinked our thought
so we deny the ways she may respond.
Let's sit in silence on the lawn
while shadows of four crows
sweep across the red-leafed trees. She speaks
in pictures, leading us away from avarice and war.
Those of us who believe
she needs our voices
will be here along the river.

The Powwow Crowd

—for Heather R. Whiteman

Punky invisibles dance. Germ, mold
and virus, quark and radical ray
spin in cycles beyond our measure.
Peer at them playing and they
find a Grand Entry song you expected.

Familiar elements dance. Soil
and water, fire, rock and air
flash and glitter without four flags.
Although they're solid to our senses,
their leaping stretches wider than our love.

Plants taught us to dance. Fern
and rush, herb and flower, elm
and moody willow reach subtle rhythms
in the wind, team dancing
with each greening cycle of the earth.

Grouse and trout, bear and human being
dance to endure. The oldest prayer's
a drum we hear in the summer
sunlight. With its beat
we honor the lightning in our blood.

Planets also powwow. Earth and moon,
one in blue fringe, the other, yellow, kick-step
with a clever wobble. Jupiter struts
among his moons while Venus
jingles round in solar wind.

The sun, a fancy dancer, balances,
then swerves his flares on this rim
of whirling stars. Differences delight
him in his timeless trance. Any comet
coming in, he'll bring along.

See the edge of it at midnight?
A skirt woven with multitudes of stars.
Serpent Skirt's harmonic hum
quickens all the dancers, releasing them
from contradictions.

I believe other galaxies join in, until
it's like the powwows down in Stroud. What
are nebulae but smoke drifting from campfires?
The drum is far away, but they sing so loud,
it booms in the center of my chest.

Cicadas

NEW POEMS

Mother's Only Daughter

Mother loved you more than she loved us,
heart of earth with the autumn sun inside.
The three of us sisters knew you
lulled her Choctaw hunger, you,
the creamy white flower she stroked on calmer days.
You trembled under the full moon near the sultry streets
of Natchitoches and Saddle Tree, then
acted innocent while she dug peanuts
under solemn pines.

She kept you well hidden in the back
of the bin, but we knew a yam
was the only real daughter, well-behaved,
adaptable and sweet, the right color, not brown
but golden, and with enough of her heat, you
mastered her tricks. You pulsed in soil

and fit her palm. We pulsed on top
and ruined her plans. If you weren't rooted,
capable of rot, your swelling would have given
her cause for alarm. She would slip off your coat
and tell us stories of all those who had you
in their grip, how you freed them, fed them,
loved them true.

You store the memory
of her fierce cuisine, that pan of hot southern fried
popping as it flew, glasses bouncing off
counter tops, shattering, shambles springing up
for us to live through them. Smelling you,
I come to the full measure of my childhood,
tasting its gold strength and letting the rest fly.

Hubert Moon's Dilemma

Snakes wiggle out the strict mazes
of their skins. Grackles cover trees
with a din of voices, lighting on branches,
cackling messages, flying
on a single groove they follow
through the field. Hubert never found
his song, even though some rhythms
are easy to latch onto. Not for him,
torn from day and night,
living a permanent evening at the home.

Once he wanted to bay at the gibbous moon,
to go where he could settle
in cool sheets, but he couldn't fathom
the direction. He kept his arms close
to his chest, just in case. Who can say
what word arrests an earthquake?
What sound could sunder wind
long enough for him to find his way?

Everywhere he heard that word—
rotunda. This world was a rotunda
and the closest he could come to the feel
of its meaning was a box canyon
he played in as a boy. Its orange walls
sifted globs of sun. The shadows
chained to leaves were dark enough
to bring on shivers. He wanted
his old days back when autumn ran
ragged over rolling hills.

His gut crusted by doubt and fear
he wondered how wolves discovered
the moss-colored star that made them sing
or how they taught their cubs
to respect the pack.
No one he loved ever came back.
Why he could not say. He watched years
turn in his hemisphere of quiet,
wishing for fences and bright stars.

Elegy for Bobby

In Memory of Robert Penn, Lakota artist

Listen. I'm carving a cleaner moon,
one without shadows, one that won't disappear
like you did on the other side of the sky,
one in whose full orange reflection
I'll see you walking down Seventh Avenue
like you did those February days when grime
got the best of us. Your voice on the phone,
its breathy pauses like you just said something
that surprised you too, hung in the air
of my green house near the creek on Ray Road.
Back then, I drove through rain, leaving
my minuscule res on a whim to wait
in some grim bar with wide brown siding
and yellow neon signs. Just when
I gave you up for good, you showed,
looking up as you came through the door,
taking a final drag from your cigarette,
your wary black eyes brightening my drink
like zesty shots of lemon. When you saw me,
the quizzical way your straight brows furrowed
moved me so much, I stayed every time.

Listen. You didn't have to go that way
into coma, letting paint make toxic
combinations of light and shallow breath.
Back then I gathered your stalwart strength
in my arms. The way you stood made it seem
you would take life in your artist's hands forever.
You planned to paint each canvas blue, wanting

the color for rescue, like it did when you were five.
Remembering a precise moment on the porch
when Cerulean breathed its truth,
you wanted to drink color, air and distance
like the true grace it is. Through you, Bobby,
that color found our world.
One moment in those fumbled meetings,
you sized me like a painting in progress. I touched
your rough face. Its fragile rhythms warmed
my hands with words. What plied
beneath our alcoholic haze was not love,
we laughed, because a bull and an octopus
could never fall in love. Ah, why did you have
to go that way?

Listen. I'm dreaming a deeper self,
one beyond stubbornness and judgment.
My impetuous inky energy disciplined
by strife, my awareness crisp as the snap
of a sheet, my heart raw and soft,
I remember how intense your life became,
how you painted the plains
as if cantilevered to the sky.
We've got the spaces you gave us,
delicate as puffs of breath in winter,
strong as the blue stars in Vela
smoky bright in a field glass.
The moon still rises. The creeks still flow.
Wet trunks darken with February rain.
I would have waited again to offer you
the hope that is also our heritage.
Now my unsettled hands simply miss
your beauty, whorled like a shell
beneath this mere current of words.

Silences

Little by little, flecks of snow fall
on boughs of massive pine.
You grip the wheel of our humming car,
heading I don't know where,
from west back east, always going
without enough cash to get there.
We do not speak. I can't say,
"Stop, let's feel these flakes
hang in air before they fringe
our lashes." I want water this way,
not muscle-bound currents
or ropes the shimmering rain uses
to rappel from cliffs of sky.
I want to learn their secret—break
from bauble to star, gather
a crowd that can comfort
a forest of hunter green.

In the cloister of bucket seats,
an iridescent dash, nothing
moves between us. I should be a duck,
stranded in a marsh, waddling
on splinters of ice. Some day
I'll risk my voice in moments of no wind,
when water is transforming into stars,
thrown in such a way
we'll never grow aware
how soon we'll both go blind.

Treatment

The main road led to a facade
of large blue squares, rows of bolted windows,
one with teddy bears. You follow the man
who plans your treatment. I stay positive
down the yellow hall, past nesting finches,
the wings of other wards,
the elevator opening on cue.
In her wheelchair, the old woman gazes
at the unsteady flames of her fingers.
Pushing her along, the old man drags
a shy leg, calls her honey.
Somewhere a woman's chanting, Help me!
We ride up. You look at the locked door,
shift your weight. Help me! They believe
your agitated state got calm because drugs
dim the clamor in your mind. They don't explain
the tick of tourettes, tonic-clonic seizures, or how drugs
tested three years on alcoholics will be prescribed
for thirty years or more. Not yet twenty-four,
you balk at the doldrums of regulated days.
You smile pensively, music from your Walkman
escaping the dizzy morning.
Do those vicious voices from the ether
remember the limits of one life?

Evenings when I visit, we go with the group
to smoke on the loading dock. A lucid dreamer,
your nights as clear to you as days,
you warn me of invasions.
I abide this darkness, watching panes
in the old pavilion waver under the one streetlight

and hear vulnerable shadows of crones
crying, Help me! Teasing me, you laugh about how
you plan to be average. I should have named
you George, so you could laugh when the crowd laughs
and not be afraid you'll break down weeping.

Months later, light graces your eyes,
although you still pace halls our Indian ways
won't reach. Time's their greatest measure.
Is it a great healer? Your days and nights
are sedated with the freight of Western expectations.
They say your illness
creates a long malaise and lack of motivation.
Do you hear the robin's medicine song,
the meadowlark's Lakota trill, warblers' steady
twitters as they return this spring?
The prairie jolts spontaneously green.
They regulate my visits, approve one gift,
reject another. Does the Indian urge to wander
itch inside your feet? What mystery jangles
in our blood? The voices never leave, but stay hushed
on the indigo rim of sound.

I believe in healing,
in the dance of sky and pigeons that rare day
we watched them circle overhead.
The wheeling flock passed at least ten times,
until you said, the lost bird finds his way.
That evening, I found it hard to leave
with Venus shining in the crushed blue sky,
Jupiter swinging in retrograde one lifetime
and rivers drying up
while the wars you dread go on.

Watching Folks Come Through

Old woman with your dog, stirring
your pot in *Maka Sica*, you expect him
to wake and eat the stew you cook.
I heard about you in Kyle where the tops
of old mountains look molded to their cores,
bones of earth reminding us
the old woman's dog could wake,
eat up the stew and end the world.

Driving through, they see the warning:
Do not get out of your car and travel far
through here; hypothermia happens
when you least expect it to. A bitter
wind blasts body heat away,
even though the sun is shining
and it looks good enough to run.

These curious organic hills
look like piled-up donut holes.
Tourists in their cars travel too fast
to see ancient spirits perched
on top peering down at them.
You sit down on a rock inside
a canyon with your pup, watching
what they acquire while gas exhausts
good air. They buzz along
not noticing strong gusts
shaking grasses on those far slopes,
same as when buffalo ambled over sage.

What obstacles will slow them down?
Already he's yipping in his sleep.
Yip, yip, yip. You keep on stirring
your pot, but it makes you laugh
to think how what they drive
drives them too.

Maka Sica: Lakota phrase for Badlands

To Rose

—for Rose Hill

The music in sumac is summer sunlight
and the high tremolo of the lead singer
as the drum beats
constant as dust and whirling stars.

My sister, between us lie
fifteen rivers and a race track
and the weather here is snow and more
the same. Just when we thought
spring came, the rain grew fat
and fell twinkling on the muddy fields.

You always wanted to bear
the biggest burdens and took them
in your easy stride as you laughed
and cried against their weight.

Now your heart and body must meander
in another mode, so you can live,
my dear one. Toss your list
in a river and head east
for a month. Yes, we've all
been dispossessed and signs
of our success often seem to vanish.

Because you have the same spirit
as summer flowers, the land here
won't wake without you, Rose.
The sumac remains sullen

and his velvet buds can't break;
new songs can't struggle
against this constant snow.
Come home to the lakes
that love you, where flashes
on the waves make you raise
your arms and shout with joy.
Come home to these blue hills.

Waning August Moon

When the sun routinely sets
And words rest with the dust
Falling thick on the dresser,
When the quarter moon dissolves
And cold rain comes early, five days
At a time, I think of your name,
Breaking it over and over into syllables.
The full August moon rises over the dark thigh
Of a mountain. It hangs above the Gallatins
And answers a question in the Pryors,
The light loved by thieves
That brought us to each other.

I shut the gauze curtain
And walk through moonlight to where you lie,
Your left hand folded under your head.
You pull back the sheet and smile.
My fingers circle over your spine
Like birds above the foothills of your home.
It's difficult to learn, this language of touch.
Ten miles up the mountain,
Snow turns into water, two crystals at a time.
We looked and could not look completely,
Fearing something may go wrong,
A trickster in the shadow.

Something will go wrong. The
Moon will wane tomorrow.
You secure the jack, check the oil,
And mention a sick wife, eight adoring children.
What choices will I have? Virgins never walk
Toward men in moonlight. I'll admit
I've wrecked homes since sixty-eight.

Professionals give you one clean break.
The motto on my card: You won't miss them,
Even once. What choices? Like water
Down the long slide of a rapid
Never leaps the same way twice,
So I want to dance and live, to move and breathe.
I rocked shut for years in a fog-bound country.

There on happy days I waited for dinner
Near a humming fridge. I hated the interior,
And stumbled through squalls on a concrete breakwater,
Helping others home. I lived a mute boulder,
Facing a sea beyond boat and cable,
Erased by the blind, indifferent sand.
One night I woke numb and heard my nakedness
Say to the moonlight, Enough shame,
Enough denial. The dust blows away,
And this arm's an arm, not wing or spider leg.
The footprints that we leave
Only sometimes fill with rainbows.

You will never know I dared
To spring the tumblers in your glance.
It's difficult being real,
Needing moons and names and people.
Needing to confide has kept me poor,
But I go on and risk without regret,
Knowing I'll arrive in that rare country,
With its lonely cry infrequent in the dusk.
Something will go right. In the west,
A ray of light will move through grasses
All at once. In the east,
With dark encouraging, the moon will wax again,
Big and orange above October fields.

Not Yet

the earth is not yet
a boarding school with a headmaster beating one march
and everyone following its laboring force
as they're handed blades to cut out the sun.
A blade is still a leaf to someone.
Let's not send
our children to become feed or to fuse their fire
to the greed of corporate boards. Let's
be heretics today, dancing outside earshot,
unfurling mandelbrot sets
that arrive in the air
of natural time and regeneration.
A blade is still a leaf.

The Whores of Telluride

They screwed the men who staked a claim
for silver. When silver crashed,
they snuggled in the sweaty arms of men
who palmed them gold.

Even if corsets laced them in,
they still danced wildly at the Sheridan.
Ruth called herself Yvette and saved
enough to buy a seat

in the green velvet coach, chugging home
to Hobokan. Women who lived
at the Silver Belle, now an historic site,
found different roads to these mountains,

fell on this corner into this house now
painted carnival bright. They grabbed wrought
iron rails before they slipped with easy
hips back to their rooms. Bordello,

peeking through Spanish lace, is not easier
to say than whorehouse. Sheila gazed
at Imogene Peak when the auburn-haired miner
who joggled titties every week told her

just how hard. She longed to taste water
in the red cliffs east of town. She dreamed
that gandy dancer who swung her round and round
would return any day to take her further west.

Angelina acquiesced to the life
at seventeen. Her basement room made her
so drowsy every day, even that Dust
riding in from Ouray got his piece.

Her face waned in the oval mirror
framed with golden daisies. Turning forty,
she loved the body that betrayed her every time,
loved the way it melted like candle wax

down her hips and eyes. Let the damn town
go bust again! Those men with burly thighs
denied her recognition. Didn't one turn
away, when she was the only one

who could teach him the taste of tears?
She taught tricks of the profession
to the twelve year old
whose breasts were itching into buds.

Guard your heart, you little twerp,
guard everything you sell, for ravishment
will age that wind moaning through stars,
and you'll have to pawn that place again.

One woman, lean as lodge pole pine, came
to find Popcorn Alley and rub her hand
on the wrought iron rail that rotted
her mother from inside.

Her eyes said *Yes* to the way mountains
rise higher in ecstasy than any human love.
She planned a raree show and shook
her bum at the men whose cash controlled
the valley. Just when they thought
she'd take it off, their bleary eyes ablaze,
she wore her rage, kindling such a fire,
its heat still burns a stranger in these rooms.

In the Colonial Zone

Inside *la Casa de Bastidas*
a massive rubber tree has tried to walk
away for five hundred years. His branches
drop down roots inside the soil
to bring up what lies hidden
deep down deep centuries ago.
He sends roots in air
to carry across time the weight
of their suffering.

I stand inside the plaza, counting
the fourteen arches where Taino
came to make the men of metal
choose — fruits of clear dreaming,
leaves folded with lies.
We of this world know
what they wanted.
I have died on these cobblestones streets,
when the sun, no, not the same sun whose
currents run now
inside my skin, my skin once again
alive and without stain.
His dogs ripped into my thigh
and I could not believe
how much the scent of blood incensed them.

So this, the first place of suffering
where blood ran because men of metal
knew the tide could wash the stone.
So this, the place where conquest gained weight
and grew into a power shaped

with the arm of empire.
The courtyard feels cool
underneath these trees and quaint shops
line the streets in the Colonial Zone.
Do German tourists hear stones speak of pain,
constant as the sea?
So deep the loss, the Spanish language
changed to accommodate its current
of grief. I come back
each day to see how far the rubber tree
has moved. Tomorrow my memory
stays here
in this first field of encounter.

Already I hear them arguing.
A human head is but a fruit,
grown from insolent earth that plays
equally in soil, in steel.

At Lame Deer, Montana

The gourd comes alive in the old man's fingers
when he closes his eyes and leans into prayer.
His song flutters many colored ribbons
over fire-lit faces before it rolls
through the night into sharp, sage air.

While cedar smoke billows through tipi poles,
the small of your back aches and heartaches climb
the spirals of your breath. Enough sighs
the weight of death makes your body hum.
Belly, brain, groin, arm waver in rhythm

with coals, flickering in a dark abyss.
After midnight, a woman's voice rings out
as clearly as a mountain stream
even though no woman sings.
Such warmth pours from singers and the drum.

First thunder above the lodge, then straight
down, green tongues of flame illuminate
the edge of human love. The hiss
of pitch escapes among the close conversations.
How often your memory keeps me there.

Before The Age of Reason

He dreamed the silver touch of the tooth
fairy on his pillow. After his second tooth
fell out, how little I knew the distance he
felt from his own flesh, his tooth taken away
by a fairy in the night and he was glad to have
it go, believing legs and arms
must fall off next. He might lose an arm
but gain a dollar. He did not want a body
because terror can't be checked. Pain and
confusion aren't soothed by fairies
and a quarter. He already merged
with the world by simply being aware
and he didn't care whether we thought
from common ground. Terror screwed
his socialization, you might say.
He lived in air, in clouds, in stars,
in moon and wind above the world
and began tracing a path from the elliptic
to Japan and knowing he'll need to speak
with them, he studied Japanese. He asked
for gills and duck feet and where could
he learn to bark like a dog,
deep and loud, to scare off robbers.
He was a dog with wings
who was going to fly back to his reservation.
There lived another boy, himself
with a different name, one he felt
more comfortable wearing in his bones.
That one often asks me
What was it we got
when we lost our land?

Remember

We climbed switchbacks
in delicious light, my love,
but you didn't see the light
in me and I had no skill to bring
it back. What lurked inside
the red throat of that quiet
road into mountains?
Reeds carrying
on their backs a limit
for the sky.

Lights Above Ray, Minnesota

—for Jemiah Aitch

The cabin door clicks shut. I see you
looking up at the resting place
of time. No sheet of familiar stars,
but shapes cascading through a space

so deep, you do not breathe. Purple vines,
sapphire fish, sheer magenta sands
drift and fade in a sea green storm. Is this
the way love is born? With both hands,

you reach up, running your fingers through
iridescence. When ground brings vertigo,
you get a camera to catch the glittering
dark. Beneath the pine whose branches also

reach for raining light, you feel humble
and calm. From the gates of night and day,
sacred beings spill star shine into soil.
All the while, a massive silence weighs

upon your heart. One billion light years out,
galaxies and dust exchange vast energies.
They touch and go. Human love's a dizzy reflection.
Like you, the cosmos grows pleased

when playing with zero. You told me a galaxy
forms from a thimble of night collapsing on itself.
From the peak of this sky, the top branches
of the sacred tree are quivering as they hold life

in place. We pulse with paradox,
with sweet darkness and fire that can move
through distances, gauged by more than eyes alone.
There is no edge, but always room to love.

In amber, in a glance, patterns change
or persevere one billion light years deep.
In this lower country, we might wake with hearts,
astonishing as this sky, or decide to sleep.

What do you believe humanity will do, when
new energies start to come through us?
Let's not doubt the harmony of bones, heart, breath,
and love first found in formlessness.

Lane Tells Gladstone
Belle His Story

When I put that man's head
In my mouth, a light came on
I'm telling you! My brain's a fire! All the while men
Are bustin' my back, clamberin' over my neck,
Shoutin' uh, uh, uh, HELP, Help, help,
pleading *Get Him OUTA there.*
THEY were freakin' out? Their hearts pumped
So much sweat my Jacobson's organ kicked in.

I got this look with my nose and whiskers rising up.
Yea, disgust. Too many strange smells all
At once and one of them was
Piss. They had a low-down opinion of me, believin'
I'm about to rip his head off. They never read
William Blake. Didn't they see me burning bright?

Four of them were prying my jaws open,
Shoving phone books and such
Into my mouth, jerkin' my canines with leather fists,
Snuffing my nose 'n holding my whiskers
Down so I can't size up the situation. All the while
I'm thinking, bite down? Leggo? Bite down?
I leggo. His head pops out 'n he collapses.

In that commotion, all I see is light, shining
Right here where my stripes create the sign of infinity.
See! It told me I wasn't a dog at all.
He treated me like you'd treat a dog,
Back in the day when I didn't know shit
From shinola. I'm telling you because

Even if you smell pretty ripe, you got a bad rap
At the wrong end of a rope. Wait! The cicadas
Are wuzz wuzzin' in the oaks. Tigers love days like these
When mountains gleam on the horizon
In blue winks. We've never known what to call 'em.

One day I'm gonna find that cove around
Here. It is a warm word. When I hear leaves
Flutter, I chuff at everyone going down
Life's highway and want a peaceful life. He treated me
So bad that I was down and out every damn day. He'd be
Saying I didn't know my ass
From a hole in the ground. I know my ass better'n
He knew his. He brought me from a breeder

In a state that starts with "T" and he owned me,
Lock, stock and barrel, draggin' me to construction sites
To put fear into fellas. Tigers get bought
And sold for patrol mostly. We spray a fence and nobody
But a lady tiger gonna step through that stink ground.
He wanted me to scare them, but he didn't know—
We sleep seventeen out of twenty-four hours.
I was more than he bargained for!

Shush! Too bad you died and nobody knows
Why. I'm telling you my story. You were a talker
That much I can tell. See, he treated me
Like a lover, rubbin' my body all over,
Hugging and pullin' my belly fur,
Scratching my chin and talkin' rough patter,
Telling secrets, fondling me till I purr loud as
An elevator, feeling this bond.
Purring means every kind of contact.

Why'd he call me "Lane" like
I'm his best, his only friend? Was Vic
That way before you grew up and he screwed
Your wife? You didn't know? That's hard to believe.
You wear a paper bag on your head when you were
Alive? That's tiger tease, so never mind.

I'm burning with life's fire, gazing at the moon,
Grass blades, rocks flaring with heat, a hawk high
On a current, a carcass. I never call it *self-
reflection*. I didn't know my own self. Neither
Did you, eh? You grow up in a trailer that smelled
Like shit? That rope burn's gotta
Hurt. Come here 'n let me lick it.

You're transparent, dude! Right
Above my eyes, my fur holds that same sheen.
Some say we deserve to die. I was caged from birth,
Worth a ton of cash. I should have bit his head off?
Then I'd be dead as you! Vic told your story.
You coulda put your two cents in and stayed alive.
Vic says only others know us and that is
who we are. You never howled and rolled in dirt,
Stared ten hours in a pool seekin'
a moire of self-reflection?
See these teeth? Stick around, cause what
I'm sayin'll help you through a bad review.

Trust me. When I cock my head
To listen, old as I am, remember I'm not a dog.
I made that point, opening
THIS wide. Agh! A yawn! That summer we
Were swimmin' in the sea 'n I held him under

A wee bit long. Yea, stupidity!
No self-reflection. Little tin gods taste deliciously
Human, but I'm no man-killer. He's in my mouth
When a light musta lit up in his head too, because
When he was free, he drove me over here
To Turpentine Creek Wild Animal Refuge and dumped
Me off. I put my belly in this warm dirt
And slept with relief. It took a long time to learn
My yellow eyes, brain and symmetry
Spring from Love. Blake calls it "burning".

As he was leaving, that fella whispered to me,
I'm never going to see you
Again. That cracks these tigers up, his talking
Like I was his woman. HE
Didn't know shit from shinola. We roar in the morning
To cure all kinds of pain. After you're dead, you still
Live in all who knew you. That's plain as whiskers.
Smell that lake northwest of here? Not even five
Miles away. I could get there some day. Living
In this luxury cage, no manacles cuff my mind. I
Roar and ROAR in the joy of knowing
What I was born for, my navel and the earth springing
From the same truth. Wake up is what I'm sayin'
And value the power of your own sweet mind.

With Fog, Falling Earthward

Loneliness engulfs me like a bright summer fog
when I see his picture and he comes alive
with easy laughter, teasing eyes, hidden heart.
Green wind, jamming down mountains, help me survive

when I see his picture and he comes alive
on this planet, whirring through the dark.
Green wind, jamming down mountains, help me survive
my wild estrangement, feeling love's a spark

on this strange planet, whirring through dark
while crickets fiddle songs along the creek.
They brim with wild estrangement, each one sparks.
I won't drop to the earth, sobbing, and be weak

when crickets fiddle songs along the creek.
He doesn't believe love is a crossroad and a tie
between dropping down forever, feigning weak,
or accepting life is rapture and good-bye.

He doesn't believe love is a crossroad and a tie.
Dragon-blue night. No moon. No drifting dialogue.
I feel my love, this rapture, this good-bye,
this loneliness seizing me in bright summer fog.

Cicada

—for Ernie Whiteman

1.

Before you left our pillows, this bed
to drive to the Twin Cities, you showed me
a cicada, fresh from its thrall of seventeen years.
The brown hull hung on your tire tread,
while the green being, too tender to fly,
trembled with the weight of gossamer wings,
struggling to adjust to the brightness of its time.

You carried him to the alder tree
whose leafy shadow made the yard an arbor.
After you left, his buzz song eased me
through lonely afternoons of sun and wind.
Desire changed his skeleton.
Desire—that green shoot in a gut.
That tendril twining with memory until new life emerges
on the opposite side
from where we first supposed. He lured his mate
to the arbor. Even after you were gone,
all the years you loved me
still sounded.

2.

I walk the smudge-colored hills
as sun lifts icy rime to mist, mist to thinning cirrus,
then the sky bolts hard blue, foretelling deeper cold.
Today your voice spiraled hoarse
with feeling over the phone.

I dreamed myself beside you,
touching the cool wash of your skin,
resting my head in the hollow of your shoulder,
your heart beating loudly against my eager ear.
I long to drink the wonder of your warmth,
your body near and certain as this sun.

3.

Cold autumn rains we argue
with ghosts inside our car.
Flicking off and on, tail lights punctuate our replies.
By spring, on humid nights, I sit in a darkened room,
stricken by chafing irritations.
On mornings, anxiety spills over the margins
of our faces until we recognize
between us the hurt some couples never lose.
We flake away our anger. It may yet
come between us, although
I pray each time we'll dig inside
for roots to keep love green and twiggy.

4.

I've been a distracted wife
scattered by the minute trials of city living.
Parking tickets I lost will lead
to our arrests. All night
I flounder in the swells of office buildings,
in currents glimmering with faces
that belong either to neon or grouper.
My spirit wanders down a spiral stair,
returns to her home on the floor of the sea.
She opens the trapdoor
beneath the puckered sand and retreats

to a forested land before her earth-time.
There hawks whistle as they fold.
There mountains thick with mist
remember her first name. Your voice calls
to her fathoms above in a raging world.
You see, beloved, I had to leave grids and squares
where heartaches glisten in shards of glass.
I had to reach the underground.

5.

We aren't blood, bone, matter,
but filaments born in the tide, coiling toward life.
At every moment, desire saunters
through those passages you've painted.
There in the dark, the flash of fireflies,
neon glowing in moon wash, caches of memory
arriving far from our human ways of knowing.
Dreamers with moth-bright eyes
and furrowed cheeks gather in my living room.
See this common stone, now look,
a shaft of sun, a nudging wave. Truth
takes a path of wonder in a world where spirits enter.

6.

You want a wall of glass where dark and light explode.
You love the rag-stock folks who wrap themselves
in rasping wind on Robert Street.
You love the sirens of St. Paul, its easy women.
I want fields of corn that rub whispers
in the sun before next equinox.
I need waves of blackbirds, chittering in trees
October afternoons. They descend and scour eaves,
the wide swathes of still green grass

until I'm forced to find the meaning
of their iridescent hoods,
of the niggling intent in their black-yellow eyes.
These hills in autumn haze
already take the weight of winter.
I can't believe how long
I've gagged on civilization.

7.

Patience is hard to practice there
in dense angles of distraction.
Dreamers want our blood to endure
even if you, dear mountain, can't shake off
the deaths they've always offered us, bottles
with despair that mutilate our spirits,
the way they program us to expect a sloppy end,
played tragic on their screens, pretending death
inevitably finds guardians of earth before
they reach their purpose. I'm not first
to go claim as kin
the cicada. Now years of silence
between us. Some day we'll greet the strangers
we'll become, stranger even now the rooms
we once called home.

A Sudden Loss of Altitude

When a weather front finds the orange voice
of its thunder, lakes shimmer, flash turquoise
and you swear you hear
down on that road along the river, music
from an all-night party, beckoning you back
to this dancing earth.

Asking the Ocean God for Release at Myrtle Beach

I waded into waves surging one after another,
translucent green blue, their warmth breaking on my calves,
knees, thighs. One green-tipped coil broke
against my belly; another doused my breasts, neck and hair.

I asked the ocean god for release
from this love, this longing for a man whose far heart
would never reach mine. The salt on my lips tasted faintly
like semen, while waves pushed me down and along,

slamming into me from my toes to my mouth
again and again. I pushed into them, rushing
as they tipped, wanting to feel them in every cell,
to sway in their energy until I became

whole in my heart, my blood, my life into that distant life,
rocking while we coil up, rocking when one breaks,
covering me with foam, blinding me
as I sank, laughing in the surges.

Release me from this love, I shouted. His name
skimmed the breakers, as the ocean god made it glisten
above the salt spray, had it hovering
like an ancient picture-word that
once kept us warm and dry.

Then the god scooped out the sand where I stood
and I sank into the name coming

back, coming back, coming back, coming, coming,
its return echoing inside the cries of gulls,

from shells on the reef in the path of the hurricane,
echoing everywhere at once, warm on my lips,
my eyes streaming tears. I gasp with ocean knowing,
while love's powerful current still carries me along.

Getting Through

—for Sterling Plumpp

With your cognac and your pace
of playing with everyday
invention, recon-cycling melodies,
notes, riffs, arrivals and departures,
you gave me the gift
of listening to blue cadences.
So, I want to tell you that I'm
getting through another day, not
imposing my will on anyone at all.
I feel portals under fields,
in creek beds some moments when
shifting a breath, song comes
purling out. Dreams create
us, warn us how lost we're bound
to get plowing through snow,
allowing ourselves to be
squished under another's thumb.

This morning
ice was forming pickup-stick
patterns on the black pond
beneath a soft as butter sun. For
no reason at all my mother's scent
hung over me, her warm bayou country
of grits, yellow perch caught on sliver hooks
frying up for breakfast. Her papaw
often left for highway crews and worked
with men whose names hushed
a muggy morning: Rufus, Royce, Carnell.

She dreamed herself a man,
but he was not my father.

I've worked in dream hollers
that still shape my resistance
to their resentments of each other.
No woman ever loved. I learned
to parade my stuffed family: Bowwow,
Kitty, Floppy and Pearl. I married
dog with cat, toad with giraffe.
At three, you can't laugh when
marriage heats up, makes holes in the road,
earthquakes of spirit. No woman ever loved
a man. Are you washed in the blood?

We've fallen from night
to dip into Erebus and drink. The dipper's
bent, banged up, but the water's
so good I hear sweet, low voices move
as I swig the damp twilight. Warm
low voices singing on a porch
before snow dumped hollows of
heartache. No woman ever loved a man,
she said, then shifted her story,
flopping her hand, showing us how
guinea hens land in the dust
of a lost farm yard. We were jus'
getting through anotha day
without expecting love to come
sauntering like Stagger Lee
over top of yonder hill. Are you
washed in the blood of the Lamb?

Ah, you helped me feel this energy
inside, valves popping on and off, heart
pulsing, fingers snapping, pit-
uitary locking up night, ancestors coming
again into this geography
on long roads north and south
and north where brown
grasses freeze, skunk cabbage glitters
with diamonds, sun without a butter glaze.
My own pa goose-stepped in stride
through that door called "civilized,"
his music a geography of blues and boarding,
rhythm off the cuff, laughing, laughing, laughing
himself silly after she died,
laughing, singing, playing music
on the front porch in front of god and,
Sweet Jesus, laughing his grief
into his grave on wet shiny streets,
always raining, hear, in this part where
the bayou comes back through the throat
'n rides the heart in sultry rhythms. Take
your damn time. No woman ever loved a man
as much. And he's on the porch again
tonight and I never knew what he's doing
playing music, hear, inventing notes
to reach his own father, another musician,
so two men, one a spirit, take their horns
and mute the stares of neighbors—
using their own precious sweet pain. Take
that, you civilized train, and that,
you thieving evil, you and I on a long road
home. Hear all those musicians, black,
Indian, blue, shrinking Europe down

to its real size, shriveling its minute breath.
No woman ever loved a man, she said,
as much as I've loved you. On her deathbed,
doing her own solo on the self she left
in the black-eyed sea, wailing over the lonely
grim ways she got washed
in the blood of the Lamb.

Your poems, Sterling, like neon tracing
those rainy nights make me admit
Stagger Lee, my fantasy father coming,
going, playing songs, mother's hand
flopping, failing to rise. Your poems—
poultice for broken spirits, for us torn
apart, north and south of Mason Dixon
whose wire cut my voice box when we drove
south of Hannibal, Missouri. Giraffe and
tree-toad got torn apart even when married.
They wandered their lives away from each other
in the same bedroom because they couldn't
dig so deep into their music. Folks torn
away from being seen as human, ripped
in opposing directions, dream us
deeply when we cross a field
and feel these bonds beyond fantasy.
Hear their rhythms arrive in my geography
because they play as we do, just
getting through another day.

Cross Section of Solitude

You knew, Ramon, that I would love you
across this courtyard, this heavy air.
The almond trees with their pale pink flowers
hide a fierce surrender, their seed
shaped into tears. You thought me tart
and cozy until I left for the sea.
My luck was moonlight over stone.
My home shuttered even when I longed
to look back and find you
under a hot bright sky.

Ramon, I was a traveler
whose only thought was to follow
boisterous clouds or a billow of butterflies.
Then in a strange country
where they deny both warmth and bitterness,
winged alder seeds took root in my gait.
So, I wait for you to find me
once again. Disguised, I wear the weight
of an old woman, watching geese
return in a wedge

beneath a windy sky.
Three young ones lead them
half the world north.
The earth guides them forever
on her road of memory,
Ramon, Ramon.

What We Wear

What we carry inside us
moves us along
whether love
hate
dishonesty
fear
joy
clarity
it grows along the way

dream the strand
frail as gossamer lilting
in the breeze above
the creek bed

that strand of light
spirit light
waving bends upon the woof
and warp of daily action
until the cloth
fragile as starlight
is long enough
for a scarf
skirt
jacket
shroud

Far West of Your Sleep

—for Agymah Kamau

Your sleep is a river beneath pines,
a river brown, deep, clear as your eyes
when you open them tomorrow, far east
of where I lie looking for loopholes
in the ceiling. You are waterfalls and rapids
with sinuous rhythms that wear away stones.
Nothing can stop your moving through
those cities. Oh, my need for you is a blur
in the thick bank. My sleep is flux and copper
flecks in the caldron of these descending days.

Your sleep is a river, possessing its own depths,
where your heart carves one forest
on the top of one hill in that place where
mountain and sea meet each other for miles.
May nothing corrupt your heart, not even
the cracked bells and banners of its losses.
May the river slough off your pain and fear,
swirling into them the pungent scent of mica,
mist and ciphers in seaweed.

Whatever it was you wasted, whatever made you
lonely, may it now pivot and jet away.
I watch it come wheeling toward me
across this border in the hour before midnight
where memory keeps waking me up,
far west of your sleep.

This Blue Stone

—for Agymah Kamau

I'm holding this poem for you, a blue stone
in my palm, translucent as kisses or
tears; its silver-blue fires might bring us
closer despite distance, difficulties
and even more years. Its longing's a breath,
lost then found, spiraling around the earth.
Like cycles of growth—seed to stem, leaf, flower,
Fruit—the root sleeps and what seems to end
grows again. This poem pretends it's innocent—
a mere stream of words flying above clouds
or letters working with pickaxes in
hand, hammering through rock to reach your feelings,
their coats flimsy frozen leaves and you in layers
of permafrost beyond warm sea breezes.

This poem holds a power wind strong enough
to blow your composure, but you would grin
and claim you could not feel it, even though
you were wheeling through the skies. Such a will
as yours, practiced and strong from challenging
the logic of oppression, might not feel
this stone become my fingertips brushing
your brow, might not catch how my longing rifts
like a samba through your sunlight, like Miles
moving the muse by changing his key
suddenly minor and moving on in,
always. If this poem has to go striding
over supernal green fields in Bavaria,
through pubs and peaks in German towns, let it

be that way. You'll discover it's taken me
along, because it knows that every moment
beyond this one, I refuse to give up
loving you. This poem covers both of us

with waves of spindrift from tides, transforming
air into presence, hard as grit and shit
and dying. I can't hide the way
love comes in this line–so boldly, but
you won't want to feel it although it's real.
Yes, my dear, nothing will erase this poem's
wild longing and no tongue but yours can taste it
on this morning of yellow leaves and no shame.

Over Mountains

From the plane window you see
our Mother dreaming ancient stands of pine,
oak savannahs, clouds blossoming
on a slope of mountain snow,
rivers meandering without words
about how far they'll travel to end
human sorrow.

These Rivers Remember

In these rivers, on these lakes
Bde-wa'-kan-ton-wan saw the sky.
North of here lies *Bdo-te*,
Center of the Earth. Through their songs,
the wind held onto visions.
We still help earth walk
her spiral way, feeling
the flow of rivers
and their memories of turning
and change.

Circle on circle supports us.
Beneath the tarmac and steel in St. Paul,
roots of the great wood are swelling
with an energy no one dare betray.

The white cliffs, *I-mni-za Ska*,
know the length of *Kangi Ci'stin-na's* tears.
He believed that words spoken
held truth and was driven into hunger.
Beneath the cliffs, fireflies flickered
through wide swaths of grass.
Oaks grew on savannahs, pleasant
in the summer winds where deer
remain unseen.

These rivers remember their ancient names,
Ha-ha Wa'-kpa, where people moved
in harmony thousands of years
before trade became more valuable than lives.

In their songs, the wind held
onto visions. Let's drop our burdens
and rest. Let's recognize our need
for awe. South of here, the rivers
meet and mingle. Bridges and roads,
highway signs, traffic ongoing.
Sit where there's a center
and a drum, feel the confluence
of energies enter our hearts
so their burning begins to matter.

This is *Maka co-ka-ya kin*,
The Center of the Earth.

Notes on the Poems

STAR QUILT: Lakota mothers and grandmothers make star quilts for their sons and grandsons. The design is a central star created out of various colored diamond shapes. The quilts are highly valued and may be used as the space for *hanbleceya*, meaning "crying for a vision" in the Lakota language.

UNDERGROUND WATER: The source of the Jung quotations is *Memories, Dreams, Reflections* (1961). As young children, both my son and I experienced intense dreams that woke us up and caused us to seek comfort. Oneida elders told me never to wake a dreamer abruptly, because when we dream, our spirit leaves our body and travels to other realms.

IN THE LONGHOUSE, ONEIDA MUSEUM: Oneidas were one of five nations of Haudenosaunee, "People of the Longhouse" and their territories in New York State were arranged as one longhouse. From the Seneca, Keepers of the Western Door, moving east to the Cayuga, People of the Great Swamp, to the Onondaga, Keepers of the Central Fire, to the Oneida, People of the Standing Stone, to the farthest east, the Mohawks, Keepers of the Eastern Door. The longhouse stood for the Confederacy.

ELEGY FOR JIM WHITE: James L. White (1936 - 1981) was my friend and fellow poet who worked in the COMPAS Program with me. He introduced me to Jim Perlman, the publisher of my three collections. When he learned that his heart was enlarging and that he would die, he spoke with me about his eminent death and his life as a gay man. He was preparing his collection, *The Salt Ecstacies*, for its publication. Graywolf Press published it posthumously in 1981.

A Nation Wrapped In Stone: When I lived with Tony Horse Road, his grandfather, Isaac Iron Shell, grew ill and was taken to the hospital in Hot Springs, South Dakota. I wrote the poem feeling sorrow for Tony's grandmother, Susan Iron Shell. Driving from the house in Upper Cut Meat, South Dakota on the Rosebud Reservation to the hospital in Hot Springs took hours of travel to reflect and feel our grief.

Reaching Yellow River: When I learned that Verdell, my friend from Rosebud, South Dakota, had died on the Yellow River in Wisconsin, due to unknown circumstances, I kept hearing his voice in my mind. We met as students at UW-Madison.

Winter Burn: Tony Horse Road and I lived for a time at Susan and Isaac's Sioux 400 at Upper Cut Meat on the Rosebud Reservation. We hauled water and chopped wood for fuel. The final lines refer to an image, a day sign, in the Mayan and Aztec calendars. The image of "one reed," refers to an image of rebirth, being the birth date of Topiltzen Quetzalcoatl, according to the Florentine Codex.

Midwinter Stars: Deer women in Plains and Woodlands mythology meet hunters. They look like human women, but their feet are hooves. They beguile hunters in order to slash the hunter with their hooves. The hunter becomes the one hunted.

The Recognition: In some American Indian mythologies, Coyote is an ancient trickster figure who acts from our human capacity for cruelty, deception, ignorance and lust, and who represents the margins of any social order. His mistakes are both comical and sometimes beneficial to human beings. All in all, his trickster ways teach people to be aware of self-deception.

Made Of Mist: The title is a play on the name of the boat that takes tourists under the falls at Niagara, New York: The Maid of Mist. The lines, "ferns hiding a lair/ where a snake lay twisted into stone./ To-morrow, even this, a darkened wound" refer to the story of the falls origins in Arthur C. Parker's *Seneca Myths and Folk Tales* and the 21,000 tons of toxic waste that Hooker Chemical buried in Love Canal.

Woman Seed Player: The title comes from the experience of seeing Oscar Howe's painting, "Woman Seed Player," when I had the chance to meet him in Vermillion, South Dakota. My friend, Bobby Penn, a protégé of Oscar Howe, took me to meet him and we talked about poetry and painting. The painting can be seen at this web site: http://groups.creighton.edu/sfmission/museum/exhibits/games/howe_09.html

Where I Come From: The quotation is from Lucy R. Lippard's *Mixed Blessings: New Art in Multicultural America* (1990, 2000). While I enjoyed the book, her comment compelled me to respond to the disputed theory of Indigenous peoples of the Western Hemisphere being "immigrants" from Asia. The theory obscures our tribal origin stories and delegitimizes Indigenous sovereignty.

Acknowledgement: Reading Rigoberta Menchu Tum's testimonial memoir, *I, Rigoberta*, I felt deeply how we are implicated in the suffering of other Indigenous peoples. I've read about Mayan culture and referred to several Mayan gods and goddesses as well as images from other sources, such as *The Popul Vuh* which tells the story of how the twin heroes are reborn as children of *Izquic*, daughter of one of the Lords of Death.

One More Sign: My uncle, Norbert Seabrook Hill, believed in mystical traditions and practiced intuitive readings. He was also a tribal politician who envisioned ways for Oneidas to become economically self-sufficient. The lines "One more sign/ an island will rise in the Caribbean." and "Some moments,/ it seems I only need to call/ to ask how ball players will arrive/ from their court beneath the waves." refer to his belief that the world would be changed through the emergence of an island rising in the Caribbean. He believed the Caribbean, including the Yucatan, held sites of ancient knowledge that would return to restore Indigenous knowledge. He urged us to pay attention in order to recognize the cultural sea changes.

PHILADELPHIA FLOWERS: Researching my grandmother's early life in Philadelphia, I saw an incredible number of poor people of all ages, races and ethnicities in the "City of Brotherly Love." Part I refers to Lucretia Mott, a Quaker abolistionist, women's rights and social justice advocate. Longhouse sachems came to Philadelphia to discuss the Confederacy and pointed out the need for sharing wealth and power, one of a number of moral grounds that was not included in framing the U. S. Constitution. Part II refers to the death of Leroy Shenandoah, a Mohawk ironworker.

EMPRESS HSAIO-JUI SPEAKS HER MIND: This persona poem creates the voice of Lady Zheng, the favored concubine of Wanli Emperor (1572-1620). In his final 20 years, Wanli squandered money for his own self-indulgence and rejected imperial duties which led to the downfall of the Ming Dynasty. Our tour guide explained that Wanli was "a party animal" in the later years of his reign. Hsaio-Jui met the young Emperor when she was fourteen and was his favored concubine throughout his reign. He became Emperor when he was nine, not ten. When I went to China on a writers' exchange program sponsored by UCLA, we toured the bathhouse he built for this woman. I was told her name was Hsaio-Jui, but cannot confirm it. We toured Dingling Tomb, including the two underground mausoleums that once held his body and that of the first Empress Xiaojing. The dragon symbolized the Emperor; the Phoenix symbolized the Empress. He wanted

Lady Zheng to be Empress, but court bureaucracy prevented it. While she was not crowned Empress until 14 years after her death, in her lifetime, she wielded considerable influence as the Emperor's favorite.

Preguntas: I was fortunate to take a course in Liberation Theology with Professor Hernan Vidal at the University of Minnesota. Professor Vidal, a Professor in the Department of Spanish and Portuguese Studies and the legal representative of the Institute for the Study of Ideologies and Literature, taught the dangers of the national security state and the need to struggle for justice and human rights which was evident during the Walleye War in Wisconsin.

Speaking With Mother: Rebecca Belmore, an Anishinaabe-Canadian Artist, came to the Twin Cities to perform her artwork, "Ayum-ee-aawach Oomama-mowan: Speaking with Their Mother" in which she spoke through a beautifully created, large megaphone which projected her voice from one of the high cliffs above St. Paul into downtown St. Paul and nearby neighborhoods. She spoke to the earth. People in St. Paul unaware of the performance might have heard a woman's voice speaking from "out of nowhere," as if the earth were speaking with them. The "megaphone" is one of the pieces in an expensive, ongoing legal battle with a Toronto gallery; please check the Rebecca Belmore Legal Fund on Facebook.

Elegy For Bobby: Robert Penn, Sicangu Lakota/Omaha Artist, (1946 - 1999) was my dear friend who I met through his cousin, Bernadine Broken Leg. When I moved from Rosebud, South Dakota, to Oneida, Wisconsin, Bobby lived and worked for the Little Red School House in St. Paul. We'd meet either in St. Paul or he'd come to visit me in Oneida. For more information on his life and work, see http://aktalakota.stjo.org/site/News2?page=NewsArticle&id=8857.

NOT YET: the line "unfurling mandelbrot sets" refers to the field of fractal geometry, created by Benoit Mandelbrot who discovered the mathematical order in the roughness of natural forms. The simple formula of complex numbers creates images of beauty found in nature, such as the patterns in cauliflowers, coastlines and human lungs.

LIGHTS ABOVE RAY, MINNESOTA: The photo this poem refers to is on Jemiah Aitch's UW site: http://pages.cs.wisc.edu/~jemiah/Photos. html. Jemiah Aitch is a computer scientist in the position of senior engineer at a logistics company in Minneapolis. The lines "You told me a galaxy/ forms from a thimble of night collapsing on itself." refers to Jemiah telling me of the discovery that observable ordinary matter (ourselves, stars and galaxies) makes up a small per cent of the energy density of the universe, while dark matter, another kind of matter entirely, and dark energy, again unknown but observable scientifically, make up the largest portion.

LANE TELLS GLADSTONE BELLE HIS STORY: This persona poem refers to two stories, Lane's and Gladstone Belle's. Lane is a tiger at Turpentine Creek Wildlife Refuge: http://www.turpentinecreek.org/. His story and the other animals' stories are posted at the refuge. Kept by a man who "treated him like a dog" until he became too much tiger to handle, his story resonated in me. He is a large tiger, but didn't kill anyone. He reflects on his life by speaking to Gladstone Belle, the main character in Agymah Kamau's second novel, *Pictures of a Dying Man* (1999), a man no one truly knew. See http://www.coffeehouse-press.org/1999/09/pictures-of-a-dying-man/.

THESE RIVERS REMEMBER: The poem refers to the Dakota villages and way of life before white settlement, along with a reference to the Dakota-U. S. War of 1862. The Science Museum Park Project incorporated lines of poems written by poets from communities of color into the small park on Robert Street in St. Paul. Dr. Chris Mato Nunpa taught me the Dakota words. He graciously corrected my spellings and provided the following translations of the Dakota words. The word, *Bde-wa'-kan-ton-wan*, the name of one of the fires of the Isanti (Santee) Dakota, means "Dwellers by Mystic Lake". The Dakota word, "I-mni-za Ska" translates as "white cliffs" and is the Dakota name for St. Paul. "*Kangi Ci-stin-na'*" means "Little Raven" and refers to the warrior and chief, who was called "Little Crow" the leader of the conflict. "*Ha-ha Wa-kpa*" has one possible translation as "River of the Falls" and refers to St. Anthony Falls. The Center of the Earth, "*Maka co-ka-ya kin*" or "*Macoke Cocaya Kin,*" is the confluence where the Minnesota River meets the Mississippi. Dr. Mato Nunpa explained that it can also be translated to mean "the Center of the Universe" which fits in with the notion that the Dakota came from the stars. The confluence is a sacred place which is also called, "Bdo-te" translated "Mendota".

About the Author

Roberta J. Hill, formerly Roberta Hill Whiteman, is an enrolled member of the Oneida Nation of Wisconsin. A poet, fiction writer and scholar, her poetry has been published in magazines, anthologies and literary reviews for many years.

For her first two collections, *Star Quilt* (1984) and *Philadelphia Flowers* (1996), published by Holy Cow! Press, she used her married name, Roberta Hill Whiteman. Her most recent poetry appears in *Sing: Poetry from the Indigenous Americas*, edited by Allison Hedge Coke (Sun Tracks, 2011); *Bringing Gifts, Bringing News*, edited and printed by George Roberts (DownStairs Press, 2011); the Black Earth Institute blog, *Thirty Days Hath September: Good Noise from the Black Earth Institute*, edited by Patricia Spears Jones, (http://lhdwriter.wordpress.com/30-days-hath-september-good-noise-from-the-black-earth-institute/); *Visiting: Conversations on Cultural Practice and Native American Art*, edited by Nancy Mithlo (2009); *Valley View: A Literary Review* (2009); *Revista de poesia Prometeo XVIII*, An anthology of poetry from the Festival International de Poesia de Medellin (2008) and *The Cold Mountain Review* (2005). Recent short fiction has been published in Sharon Holland and Tiya Miles, *Crossing Rivers, Crossing Worlds, The African Diaspora in Indian Country* (Durham: Duke University Press, 2006); *The Deadly Writers Patrol*, #5, 2007; and *Pow-wow: charting the fault lines in the American experience: short fiction from then to now,* by Ishmael Reed and Carla Blank (Philadelphia, PA: Da Capa Press, 2009). Roberta Hill has read her poems throughout the United States, most recently in Minneapolis, Minnesota and Manitowoc, Wisconsin, and at International Poetry Festivals in Medellin, Columbia and the Poesia Do Mundo in Coimbra, Portugal, as well as in China, Australia, New Zealand.

Hill is a professor in the English Department and in the American Indian Studies Program, with an affiliation in the Nelson Institute for Environmental Studies at the University of Wisconsin-Madison where she teaches courses in Multicultural Literature, American Indian Studies and Environmental Literature.